Believe!

Believe!

HELPING YOUTH
TRUST IN THE LORD

ROBERT C. OAKS

DESERET
BOOK

SALT LAKE CITY, UTAH

Aircraft photographs provided courtesy of the United States Air Force.

Library of Congress Cataloging in Publication Data

Oaks, Robert C.
   Believe! : helping youth trust in the Lord / Robert C. Oaks.
      p.   cm.
   Summary: Through personal experience and stories, shows how trusting in the Lord and following his direction leads to satisfaction and happiness, while ignoring his counsel leads to disappointment and unhappiness.
   Includes bibliographical references and index.
   ISBN-10 1-59038-203-X (pbk.)
   ISBN-13 978-1-59038-203-5 (pbk.)
   1. Christian life—Mormon authors—Juvenile literature. 2. Youth—Religious life. 3. Church of Jesus Christ of Latter-day Saints—Doctrines—Juvenile literature. 4. Mormon Church—Doctrines—Juvenile literature. [1. Christian life. 2. Church of Jesus Christ of Latter-day Saints—Doctrines. 3. Mormon Church—Doctrines.] I. Title.

BV4501.3.O25 2003
248.8'3—dc22   2003020711

Printed in the United States of America
Malloy Lithographing Incorporated, Ann Arbor, MI

10 9 8 7 6 5 4

To my mother and father,
Ann and Charles Oaks, for their unending efforts to teach
me the higher path by example and spoken precept

To my wife, Gloria,
who has followed me and supported me across the
face of the earth throughout our thirty moves

And to our children—
Perry, Bart, Keri, Derek, Brock, and Kristie—
for their cheerful acceptance of
their nomadic upbringing

Contents

Preface ix

Acknowledgments xiii

1. Trust, Born of Disappointment 1

2. Trust in Youth 9

3. The Untrustworthy Arm of Flesh 17

4. Trust in the Lord through Prayer 23

5. Trust in the Word of God 35

6. Trust When You Cannot See 49

7. Trust in the Lord through Obedience . . . 59

8. Trust in the Law of Chastity 67

9. Trust in the Law of Tithing 73

10. Trust in the Word of Wisdom 77

11. Trust in the Lord through Service 85

CONTENTS

12. Trust in the Lord through
    Missionary Work 93

13. Trust in the Lord's Atonement 99

14. Trust in the Lord in Your Decisions 107

15. For Strength, Trust in the
    Arm of the Lord 115

    Index 121

    About the Author 125

Preface

I was raised an active member of The Church of Jesus Christ of Latter-day Saints, and I grew up in a predominantly Latter-day Saint community along the Wasatch Front in Utah. My young friends and I had the advantage of living in surroundings that taught and exemplified basic Latter-day Saint morals and values. At home and school and in Church and community, we found a healthy consistency in standards and direction. Even as I worked in my grandfather's hay field or barnyard, I was never out of sight of at least one Latter-day Saint chapel.

Despite that consistency, my friends and I faced a multitude of opportunities to veer from the gospel path and wander down dark trails to unhappy destinations. But we seldom had cause to sit and wonder, "What is the right thing for me to do in this morally challenging situation?" We were surrounded with clear messages of the Lord's preferred path.

When I entered the United States Air Force Academy as a freshman, my world changed dramatically. The consistency of values disappeared. While most of my new classmates held to basic Christian standards, some openly challenged my sense of right and wrong.

Thirty-five years of service as a pilot and a commander in the United States Air Force gave me many opportunities to see in the lives of young service members the positive results of living in accordance with basic Christian values. Conversely, I saw in the lives of other service members the destructive results of living in accordance with the standards of the world and of violating the Lord's gospel law.

As a father, I watched my six children, for whom my wife, Gloria, and I cared very much, face the same challenges that I had faced in my youth—but in a much more diverse environment. We raised our family in the Air Force, moving around the world to spots where Latter-day Saint doctrine and views were in the minority. To compensate for the lack of community consistency that Gloria and I had enjoyed in our youth, we had to provide our children with increased moral instruction in our home. Distracting peer pressure was more common for them than it had been for us. But they emerged stronger because they had to swim in a current that was made swifter by surroundings that lacked consistent support and guidance.

Having served as a district president in the Boy Scouts of America for four years and in various Church callings—from seminary teacher to stake president and now as a General Authority—I have had many opportunities to watch young men and young women encounter the challenges of life from different perspectives. From these experiences, I have become familiar with the ways young people can work through their challenges.

The young men and young women of East Africa with whom I worked from 2000 to 2003 face different challenges, but the solutions to those challenges generally come from the same source. When we believe in God and place our trust in his wisdom, love, and counsel, peace and progress will enter our lives, driving out our guilt, despair, and many other manifestations of pain and misery.

I have used many personal experiences in this book to show that trust in the Lord is essential to living a life of joy and happiness. I have not always trusted in the Lord as I should have, nor have I always made the right decisions. But I have gained a strong testimony of the bounteous blessings that flow from placing faith and trust in the Lord and striving daily to follow his example.

Trusting in the Lord and following his direction lead to satisfaction and happiness; ignoring his counsel leads to disappointment and unhappiness. It is that simple. I hope that the experiences I share, coupled with scriptural examples, will assist you young men and young women in developing trust in the Lord while you are young, relatively inexperienced, and faced with making many important decisions.

The opinions and views in this book are my own. This is not a Church publication and has not been prompted by any assignment or request from the First Presidency or the Quorum of the Twelve Apostles.

Acknowledgments

In addition to expressing my gratitude for the strong and continuous encouragement I received from my family, I must express special appreciation to Sister Geroldine Edwards for her encouragement to continue writing even when the output was discouraging. Also, thanks to the staff of Deseret Book for their patience with a novice, and to Michael Morris for his editing skills.

CHAPTER 1

Trust, Born of Disappointment

And now, O my son Helaman, behold, thou art in thy youth, and therefore, I beseech of thee that thou wilt hear my words and learn of me; for I do know that whosoever shall put their trust in God shall be supported in their trials, and their troubles, and their afflictions, and shall be lifted up at the last day (Alma 36:3).

My mother knew what had happened even before I walked in the front door. By the way I shuffled slowly up the lane to our house in Provo, Utah, she knew that I'd been cut. In high school I had certainly never been a star, but at least I had made the football team and been allowed to play a bit. The same was true for the basketball, baseball, and tennis teams. But now there was not going to be any helmet, shoulder pads, or uniform. I hadn't even made it past the first cut for the Brigham Young University freshman football team.

Like many young athletes, I thought I was a lot better than I actually was. But I had dreamed of wearing the Cougar blue and white all my life. I shouldn't have been surprised, but this was long before Steve Young, Ty Detmer, conference championships, a Heisman Trophy, and a national championship had come to the

BYU campus. This was even before LaVell Edwards stalked the sidelines. In fact, it was so long ago that Steve Young's dad, Grit, and I, who had been high school teammates, tried out together. Grit was good enough to make the team. I wasn't.

When I shuffled into the house, my mother tried to comfort me. "I know how you feel," she said. How could she? She had never been cut from a football team. In my eyes she was a first-team All-American mother, but that didn't help me a bit on that particular day.

Two months later when I went out for the BYU freshman basketball team, I experienced an instant replay. I was again cut in the first round. I was so discouraged that I didn't even bother trying out for the baseball team. My most important worldly aspirations had been dashed. The arm of flesh had let me down—a terrible blow for a would-be quarterback. I had wanted so badly to follow in my dad's All-American footsteps at BYU.

Still not understanding the limits of my arm of flesh, I started looking for new fields on which to play. The following year, 1955, the new United States Air Force Academy was planning to open. Certainly academy athletic teams could use my strong arm. Besides, enrolling in the academy would give me a chance to achieve another one of my goals: learning to fly. I applied and was accepted, knowing that my acceptance was not based on my athletic prowess. I had always done fairly well in academics and in other school activities, and that balanced record got me into the new academy.

The academy *did* have athletic teams—a lot of them—but it only had 306 cadets in that first class. The academy needed my healthy body and every other healthy body its teams could get their hands on. I made the football team, the basketball team, and the baseball team that year, but I began to realize that I was never going to follow in my dad's All-American footsteps. I was soon down to playing only football, and one day when a misstep sent my knee one way and my body another way, my college athletic dreams were over. To my great disappointment, I had discovered that the leg of flesh was even less dependable than the arm of flesh.

This little scenario is not the stuff from which tales of high drama or gripping adventure are created. But it became the foundation in my younger years for my understanding that the strength of the arm of flesh and the dreams that flow from trusting in that strength are unreliable and untrustworthy.

After graduating from the Air Force Academy in June 1959, I married Gloria Unger of Provo, and we moved to Bartow, Florida, to begin pilot training. I was no Charles Lindbergh, but I did well enough in the primary training phase to feel confident that I would be able to complete the pilot training program and wear the silver wings of a United States Air Force pilot.

We then moved to Vance Air Force Base in Enid, Oklahoma, for the second half of the yearlong pilot training course. I started out doing quite well in the initial phase of training at Vance. Consequently, when the Air Training Command Inspection Team came down to see how the flying training program was going at Vance, I was selected to fly with a member of the team.

Unfortunately, I'd had a bad formation flight earlier that day. My confidence was shot, and I was nervous. As a result, virtually every maneuver I tried to execute with the inspection team went wrong. Early on I knew that I was going to fail the flight, and I knew the importance of doing well because I had been trusted to represent the training base. Before we landed, I was sure that I would immediately be washed out of flying school and never achieve another important goal. Excelling at flying had replaced athletics as the central focus of my worldly ambitions, but once again it looked like I wasn't going to make the cut.

When we returned to the base and tried to land, I couldn't get the T-33 training aircraft on the runway. We were landing on a shorter runway than I had ever used before, and I had difficulty making the adjustment even after several attempts. I learned later that the instructor pilot who was manning the mobile control unit at the end of the runway finally said in disgust, "If we are going to get him down, we will have to shoot him down."

When I finally did get the plane on the ground, I almost ran off the end of the runway. I was mortified. When we went into the debriefing room, the inspection team pilot said to me, "If you don't like to fly, get out of the program now." That was all he said, but it was much worse than not seeing my name on the roster of the BYU freshman football team. I went home that day more crushed and disappointed than I had ever been before.

Fortunately, I had been blessed with a wise and patient instructor pilot when I had arrived at Vance Air Force Base. The next day he took me up on a refresher, confidence-building flight to let me know that he still had faith in me and my flying ability. When I finished the flying training program at Vance, I had done well enough to be able to select a fighter assignment.

Several years later I flew an audition flight with the United States Air Force Aerial Demonstration Team, the Thunderbirds. One of my prime motivations for selection was that I wanted to be able to return to that inspection team pilot with proof that I really could fly an airplane. Such a desire was childish but somewhat understandable, given the magnitude of my embarrassment for failing to perform on a day when people had counted on me to represent the base. I was not nearly as disappointed at not being selected for the Thunderbirds as I had been on that black day during pilot training.

I never forgot one of the most important lessons I learned in flight school—a lesson reiterated during my career as a pilot and after my retirement: the possessions and positions of the world are fragile and can quickly slip through our fingers. That's why we need to learn to trust in the Lord. I believe that process goes on throughout our lives—even when things are going well.

After thirty-five years in the United States Air Force, I retired. At the time, I was a four-star general in command of the United States Air Force in Europe and of NATO air forces in the central region of Europe. For my retirement, the Air Force honored me with a large change-of-command ceremony featuring flattering talks by important NATO representatives. I was privileged to inspect the troops before they marched in review past the podium. Then a flyby of jet fighters topped off the ceremony. To bring up the rear of the flyby, officials found an old F-100 Super Saber like the one I had flown in the Vietnam War. By the time it was all over, I felt quite honored and important—by the standards of the world.

Gloria and I walked down to the flight line and got on a C-141 transport aircraft, and I then flew us back to the United States, where we were to have a formal retirement ceremony the following week. On the way home, I even had the opportunity to complete an air refueling from a KC-135 tanker over the Atlantic Ocean. I was feeling pretty much on top of the world, looking forward to another impressive ceremony where all of my Air Force and Church friends living in the Washington, D.C., area would join with my family, including our four sons, who were on active duty in the Air Force, to honor me.

I landed the C-141 at Andrews Air Force Base on a Saturday afternoon, and we spent a relaxing weekend getting ready for the coming week. On Monday morning, Gloria and I started out on a short shopping trip. It felt good to hop in a car and go somewhere without security troops following us as they had throughout our four-year assignment in Europe. But as I reached for the car door handle, something stung me on the hand. We later concluded that it was a wasp or a hornet. Whatever it was, within a couple of minutes I was slumped over the steering wheel, unconscious and fading deeper and deeper into anaphylactic shock.

Gloria quickly overcame her panic, ran to the house, and called 911. Medical crews responded within five minutes and soon had me on the table of an emergency room in a nearby hospital. I lay unconscious on that table for five hours, with attending doctors expressing doubts about their ability to revive me. Gloria was alone for several hours until a friend joined her at the hospital to give her some much-needed support. The tremendous highs of Saturday had turned into some deep lows on Monday. No cheery, well-wishing friends in their crisp uniforms, no band playing for the marching troops, no roaring, saluting jets—just a frail body on an emergency room table with a prayerful, teary wife in constant attendance.

What is my "trust in the Lord" lesson from all of this? Quite simply, the high honors of men and all of the shiny, fast-moving things of the world can deeply disappoint us. They fade rapidly and mean little in the eternal scheme of things. The only meaningful treasures and honors that I had on that emergency room table that stark afternoon were those that I had accumulated in my life through acts of goodness, virtue, and kindness—the treasures of heaven. Since that day I have always tried to note which account is receiving the largest investments of my time and energy—the account of worldly honors and things or the account of spiritual growth and thoughtful deeds.

Just as the athletic goals that were so important to me proved to be elusive and disappointing, the honors of men and other treasures of the world cannot provide a sure and solid foundation for joy in this life or in the life to come. Trusting in the Lord and in his ways is the only path to true joy and lasting happiness.

POINTS TO PONDER

- The pleasures and accomplishments of the world and the honors of men are elusive and fragile and can quickly fade and disappear, leaving disappointment in their place.
- The Lord is a sure foundation for our lives and happiness.
- Trust in the Lord and in his ways and you will be rewarded with peace in your heart and serenity in your soul.

CHAPTER 2

Trust in Youth

David said moreover, the Lord that delivered me out of the paw of the lion, and out of the paw of the bear, he will deliver me out of the hand of this Philistine (1 Samuel 17:37).

You, the youth of Zion, face significant temptations and challenges, many of which were not so commonplace in earlier generations. Profanity, body defacement, drugs, pornography, immodesty, and sexual immorality are not new, but they are much more acceptable than they were a few short years ago. Their acceptance seems to represent a rejection of spiritual standards.

How can youth, caught in the turbulent crosscurrents of corruptive culture, pressing peers, pleading parents, and believing bishops, chart a course that will keep them flying above worldly dangers?

Attention to your course is important throughout your lives, but never is it more critical than during your youth, when so many of your peers press on, full throttle, without the benefit of compass or rudder. That is why you must cling to the stabilizing, direction-giving counsel to "trust in the Lord." At a time in your life when you have the greatest need of light and guidance, one who cares so deeply and knows so much is available to you. All you have to do is trust in him and turn to him.

It should be no surprise that God the Eternal Father and his Son Jesus Christ care for you deeply. God the Father is the father of your spirit. He knows you by name and by personality, and he wants the very best for you. Jesus Christ is your Savior and Redeemer, and he has proven his love by suffering for your sins in Gethsemane and on the cross at Calvary. The Father and the Son want you back in their presence to dwell with them for the eternities. Their love for you is as natural as that of a mother for her newborn baby.

An important fact that young people often forget is that the Lord loves them in general and each of them specifically. Time and time again he has shown his trust and love for youth as he has placed great responsibilities upon their shoulders. Samuel the prophet was called by the Lord as a young boy and shown a vision of the destruction of the house of Eli (1 Samuel 3:10–14). David, in like manner, was called by the Lord as a young boy and anointed by Samuel to be the king of Israel. And while still in his youth, David saved Israel from the wrath of the Philistines by slaying Goliath (1 Samuel 16:11–13; 17:32–52).

In similar fashion, the Book of Mormon also reflects the Lord's trust and love of youth. Nephi was a young man when he slew Laban to gain possession of the brass plates, had a vision of the tree of life, and received instructions on building a ship in which his family would cross the great waters to their new home-land (1 Nephi 4:16–18; 11:1–11, 21–23; 17:8; 18:1–4). Likewise,

Mormon was in his youth when he was visited by the Lord and when he was called upon to lead the Nephite armies against the Lamanites in their futile fight for survival (Mormon 1:15; 2:2).

One of the greatest examples of the Lord's trust and love of youth is found in the Joseph Smith story. In answer to Joseph's simple but fervent prayer in the Sacred Grove when he was but fourteen years old, the Father introduced the Son to him, thereby starting the glorious process of the restoration of the gospel of Jesus Christ. Because of this trust on the part of the Lord, Joseph's life was forever changed as he fulfilled his foreordained role as the prophet called to usher in the dispensation of the fulness of times.

The Lord's trust in youth as he bestows the Aaronic Priesthood upon worthy young men, starting at age twelve, is so commonplace that we often overlook it. Aaronic Priesthood holders are empowered to prepare, bless, and pass the sacrament, to teach the gospel as home teachers, and to undertake many other assigned duties. When they turn eighteen, they can be blessed with an even greater token of trust, the Melchizedek Priesthood. And shortly thereafter, they can be called into the mission field, where they are entrusted with the sacred responsibility of spreading the restored gospel "to every nation, kindred, tongue, and people" (Mosiah 15:28). In fact, the Lord has trusted the bulk of the responsibility for spreading his gospel throughout the world to young men and young women serving as full-time missionaries.

One final but magnificent example of the Father's trust in youth is his selection of the young Virgin Mary to be the mother of his Only Begotten Son. Mary may have been as young as sixteen when Gabriel appeared to her and described her divinely appointed role. In choosing Mary, the Father ignored experience, maturity, wealth, and position in favor of youthful virtue, faith, and courage. Mary was entrusted with the delivery, nurturing, and teaching of the Son of God and Savior of all mankind.

Latter-day prophets have repeatedly highlighted the special trust the Lord has in youth born in these days of the dispensation of the fulness of times. George Q. Cannon, a member of the First Presidency, stated this basic principle in 1866:

"God has reserved spirits for this dispensation who have the courage and determination to face the world, and all the powers of the evil one, visible and invisible, to proclaim the Gospel, and maintain the truth, and establish and build up the Zion of our God, fearless of all consequences. He has sent these spirits in this generation to lay the foundation of Zion never more to be overthrown, and to raise up a seed that will be righteous, and that will honor God, and honor him supremely and be obedient to him under all circumstances."[1]

President Gordon B. Hinckley reinforced this powerful vote of confidence in youth when he observed, "You really are 'a chosen generation.' You are better educated. You desire to do the right thing. Many of you are trying to keep yourselves free from the corrosive stains of the world. In so many ways, you are remarkable! You are exceptional! I believe that as a group, you are the finest this world has ever seen. It is important for you to understand that you are part of a chosen generation. Limitless is your potential. Magnificent is your future, if you will take control of it and if you will decide now that you will not let your life drift in a fruitless and aimless manner."[2]

Why, then, are you young people sometimes reluctant to trust in the Lord? Well, as children you come into this life with no recollection of your previous existence in the presence of God. You are born into a "natural man" state with appetites to bridle and selfishness to shed. It is easy for you to be distracted from focusing on your spiritual needs and on the distant horizons of adulthood and eternity.

As a young person living life to the fullest, you may naturally ask yourself, "Why are there so many rules that seem designed to take the fun out of life? Why does the Lord get blamed for so many of these rules? Why do I have to make so many important decisions about so many important things while I am so young?"

These are questions young people have asked in various forms for centuries, and for centuries, parents, teachers, and leaders have tried to provide meaningful answers, with varying degrees of success. But they are important questions, and they deserve good answers. When these questions are answered, many other concerns are also addressed.

What about rules? The most important rules are called eternal laws. They come from the Lord, and they are based on eternal truths that provide a foundation for your eternal happiness. It's important to realize that eternal happiness is much more lasting and preferable than "plain old fun." Comparing happiness with fun is like comparing a modern F-16 jet fighter to the first airplane designed by Orville and Wilbur Wright.

But the promise of eternal happiness is more complicated than an F-16 or any other airplane ever built. It involves combining concepts like premortality, the creation of the earth and of man, the fall of Adam and Eve, opposition in all things, the Atonement, repentance, forgiveness, and resurrection into a grand and meaningful masterpiece called the plan of salvation. This plan is also called the plan of life or the plan of happiness. It is not called the plan of fun, but it can be fun aligning your life with the Lord's magnificent pattern for a happy life. We just have to live our lives within the bounds of eternal law. Within those bounds exists plenty of room for good, clean fun.

When I took my first F-16 flight, I didn't run out and start tearing the airplane apart to make sure it would work. I trusted the engineers who designed and built it, I trusted the mechanics who maintained it, and I trusted the instructor pilot who prepared me to fly it. He taught me the rules of flying and helped me to understand the do's and don'ts before I ever left the ground. After I was appropriately instructed, I climbed in and lit the fire. On every flight, whether going to the gunnery range to drop bombs or performing a low-level navigation mission, I had a flight plan. Without a flight plan, I wouldn't have known where I was going or how I was going to get there.

If we are so willing to trust the engineers, mechanics, and teachers in our lives, why are we reluctant to trust God? He loves us far more than any collection of people and even more than our earthly parents. He is our spiritual creator and our Eternal Father, and he wants only good things for us, now and for all eternity. That is why his plan is called the plan of happiness. His perfect love for each of us and his desire for our welfare should certainly prompt us to trust him. Remember, he is our Father.

The questions you have in your youth about the purpose and meaning of your time on earth are complex and important. Until you find answers to these questions, you may wander into dangerous, turbulent clouds that may be hiding rocky mountain peaks. But when you find answers to your questions, you will also find meaning and direction that will help you develop a flight plan for safely returning to your Father in Heaven.

That is why it is so important that you humble yourself, acknowledge your Father, kneel before him, and look heavenward for answers. He has answers to all of your important questions if you will but ask him and wait patiently for his reply. This humbling, seeking, and waiting patiently is the beginning of trust in the Lord and faith in the power of his restored gospel. The fruits born of that trust and faith will be sweet treasures for you all the days of your life.

Our Heavenly Father and his Son Jesus Christ have repeatedly proven that they love and trust you. They want you to succeed in all of your righteous desires and enterprises, and they have prepared a path for you to follow that will lead you back into their presence. All you have to do is trust them and follow that path.

POINTS TO PONDER

- Our Father in Heaven has demonstrated time and again his love for and his trust in youth.
- The Father and Son see in young men and young women much greater potential than they see in themselves.
- Youth have repeatedly played key roles in moving the Lord's work forward.
- You should use your time to determine your foreordained role in this life and then prepare yourself to fulfill that role.

NOTES

1. George Q. Cannon, in *Journal of Discourses,* 26 vols. (London: Latter-day Saints' Book Depot, 1854–86), 11:230.
2. Gordon B. Hinckley, *Way to Be* (New York: Simon & Schuster, 2002), 3–4.

CHAPTER 3

The Untrustworthy Arm of Flesh

O Lord, I have trusted in thee, and I will trust in thee forever. I will not put my trust in the arm of flesh; for I know that cursed is he that putteth his trust in the arm of flesh. Yea, cursed is he that putteth his trust in man or maketh flesh his arm (2 Nephi 4:34).

When the great Book of Mormon prophet Lehi died, Nephi cried unto the Lord with some of the most powerful words on trust ever penned, or in Nephi's case, ever pounded. Twenty-four hundred years later, Joseph Smith would mine from the gold plates Nephi's treasured words on trust, as quoted above.

Knowing that "cursed is he that putteth his trust in the arm of flesh" sounds good, but it's hard to keep in mind when you're a strong young man who can run fast, jump high, and throw or hit a ball out of sight.

It's also hard if you're a young woman with talent, beauty, and the world at your feet. When you're young, the arm, leg, and face of flesh seem able to conquer all, and you think that strength and beauty will last forever. Alas, it is not so.

In my youth I saw a powerful example of the short life of the strong arm of flesh. My father, Charles Oaks, used to take me to BYU football games. In those days we would stand together on the sidelines behind the bench and watch the home team invariably get beaten. Three football wins made a banner year for the Cougars in those years.

Toward the end of every dismal game, someone would come up to me and say, "Bobby, what they need is for your dad to be out there knocking heads. He would show them how to play football." Dad had been an All-American player at BYU. In fact, his coach told him that he was BYU's first All-American football player. But football wasn't the limit of his athletic skill. Dad had been an all-state basketball player in high school and once had been asked to try out for a professional baseball team. I never saw him play football or basketball, but I saw him play a lot of softball, and I knew he was a great athlete. Further, as I watched Dad work while I was growing up, I realized that he was a very strong man. His arm of flesh was pretty trustworthy, or so it seemed.

In his later years Dad spent much of his spare time going to the temple to perform sacred ordinances for the living and in behalf of the dead. He worked in the temple as long as his health permitted. Eventually, standing for prolonged periods of time became too painful, and his eyesight and hearing failed him. In those years he walked slowly and not very far, even with his cane. All of his speed, strength, and agility had slipped away over the years, as it eventually does for all of us.

As I considered Dad's life, I often contemplated who would be there to greet him when he passed through the veil—football fans hollering for another touchdown or grateful souls eager to thank him for his help with their temple ordinances. I don't think there is much question as to which of his endeavors will provide the most eternal satisfaction to him.

At Dad's funeral in June 2002, each of his four children spoke, reflecting on their individual recollections of his life and on the impact he had had on his family and friends. It was interesting to note that little was said about his athletic accomplishments. Instead, he was lauded for living by eternal gospel principles—exemplary hard work, dogged self-reliance, constant willingness to assist others in time of need, deep love of his family, and an abiding care and concern for his children. Dad never had any hobbies or pastimes that did not include his family.

As my siblings and I spoke, we dwelt on our memories of spending time with Dad and on how much he had taught us about working and serving, fishing and hunting, and so forth. The priorities of Dad's life reflected the trust he had developed in the Lord by building his character on the basic tenets of the gospel of Jesus Christ.

An impressive example of the folly of trusting in the arm of flesh is found in 1 Samuel 17. The story of David and Goliath provides a dramatic illustration of the contrast between the power of trusting in the Lord and the power of trusting in the arm of flesh. Goliath was a giant of a man with all of the protecting armor and threatening weapons that the mind could devise. So great was his trust in his own physical strength that he gambled the freedom of his army and of his people on his ability to kill in hand-to-hand combat any man that the Israelites might put up against him.

Goliath's boasting went on for forty days, until David heard it. He was deeply offended by Goliath's brash assertions, defying "the armies of the living God" (1 Samuel 17:26). Trusting in the power of the Lord, which had delivered him from a lion and from a bear that were ravaging his herd of sheep, David decided to go forth to battle the giant. The drama of that moment must have been remarkable to behold: David, an armorless youth, confronting a seemingly unconquerable giant. But David was not impressed with the fleshy disparities.

"Then said David to the Philistine, Thou comest to me with a sword, and with a spear, and with a shield: but I come to thee in the name of the Lord of hosts, the God of the armies of Israel, whom thou hast defied. This day will the Lord deliver thee into mine hand; and I will smite thee, and take thine head from thee; and I will give the carcases of the host of the Philistines this day unto the fowls of the air, and to the wild beasts of the earth; that all the earth may know that there is a God in Israel. And all this assembly shall know that the Lord saveth not with sword and spear: for the battle is the Lord's, and he will give you into our hands" (1 Samuel 17:45–47).

That, of course, is exactly what happened. David rushed forward, took a stone from his pouch, and flung it with his sling, burying it in the forehead of the menacing giant. After David cut off the fallen warrior's head, the army of Israel routed the Philistine army, driving them from the field. Thereafter for many years, David put his trust in the Lord and prevailed in his numerous battles defending the cities and citizens of Israel.

The strength of the arm of flesh will inevitably fade and disappear, as it did with my father, or completely fail in a moment, as it did with Goliath, but the strength of the arm of the Lord will endure and sustain all those who embrace gospel truths with their trust, obedience, and service. The scriptures are full of examples of the blessings that flow into the lives of those who put their trust in the strength of the Lord. They are also full of painful stories of those who put their trust in the strength of the arm of flesh and lightly regard the Lord's offering of blessing and protection to those who follow him.

POINTS TO PONDER

- No mater how high the mountains we climb or how bright the lights illuminating our name, one day the books recounting our worldly greatness will gather dust on a forgotten bookshelf.
- No matter how insignificant we feel, the books recounting our acts of trust, obedience, faith, and service will be noted and acclaimed far beyond our mortal lives.

CHAPTER 4

Trust in the Lord through Prayer

And whatsoever ye shall ask in my name, that will I do, that the Father may be glorified in the Son. If ye shall ask any thing in my name, I will do it (John 14:13–14).

The gem of trust has many different facets. One of the most lustrous and gleaming of those facets, and one of the most valuable for you in your youth, is the facet of prayer. It is impossible to come to a position of strong trust and faith in the Lord without regular recourse to personal prayer. The scriptures are filled with admonitions to pray and with promises of the glorious blessings that will flow to you when you seek the Lord's help and assistance through prayer.

In the New Testament, the Savior makes a remarkable promise when he states, "And whatsoever ye shall ask in my name, that will I do, that the Father may be glorified in the Son. If ye shall ask any thing in my name, I will do it" (John 14:13–14).

This glorious promise is not limited to the New Testament. Through his prophet Jeremiah, the Lord admonished Israel, "Then shall ye call upon me, and ye shall go and pray unto me, and I will hearken unto you. And ye shall seek me, and find me, when ye shall search for me with all your heart" (Jeremiah 29:12–13). In like manner, he will respond to your sincere, heart-felt prayers.

In my life I have seen the sweet fruits of faithful, diligent prayer in navigating my way through some difficult and trying situations. In 1965 I headed to Vietnam for my third tour of duty. At the time I was assigned to the 416th Tactical Fighter Squadron, the Silver Knights, stationed at Tan Son Nhut Air Force Base on the outskirts of Saigon. We were flying combat missions just about every day, with our squadron's F-100 Super Sabers taking small arms hits regularly. Although the air war in South Vietnam was dramatically less hazardous than the air war being fought in the skies over North Vietnam, we still faced enough enemy fire to make our hearts race a bit. In this environ-ment, I easily developed faithful habits of prayer, and I found strength in knowing that my family back home was praying reg-ularly for my safe and speedy return.

Looking back, I can see clearly that these prayers helped build a protective shield around me. I felt this protection especially on the morning of March 30, 1966. At about 5 A.M., one of my squadron mates came to my room, woke me up, and asked me to take his flight, which would start with a 6 A.M. briefing. He had stayed up too late partying and was in no shape to fly. Since I loved to fly anytime, I told him to go back to bed. I jumped up and rushed to the briefing. Because I was scheduled to lead a flight of four F-100s, I had to get to the flight operations building a bit early to prepare to brief the other pilots. The target area was one we had hit regularly in the Mekong Delta, so it didn't take too much target study and navigation planning to get ready.

The takeoff and flight into the target area were uneventful, and we quickly made contact with the on-scene "forward air controller." He warned us about enemy troops hidden in banana trees along the edge of a rice field and then directed us to selected targets. About halfway through our mission, I pulled off from a strafing pass and noticed that my fire warning light had lit up. I had been hit! I was in trouble, so I headed east toward the nearest friendly airfield—a little asphalt strip called Soc Trang. I don't know what I thought I was going to do with my big jet when I got to that short field, but I wanted to get away from the target area as rapidly as possible.

I was feeling pretty good about things until my wingman, Lt. Joe Westenhaver, told me that I was burning badly, with flames trailing several feet behind the aircraft. A moment later, the aircraft quit responding to the control stick. It was time to bail out. I raised the armrest in preparation for blowing the canopy off the aircraft. As soon as the armrest was clear, I squeezed the trigger, firing the ejection seat charge. It fired much more violently than I had expected, but at least I was separated from the burning F-100. Later I would require an operation to fuse two vertebrae in my spine as a result of being ejected from the seat, but right then a little back pain was the least of my worries.

As soon as I ejected, things quickly went from bad to worse. The jolt of the ejection put me into a rapid, head-over-heels tumble. The tumble was so violent that I couldn't think through the remainder of my memorized emergency procedures. My only clear thought at the time was that the human body was not built

25

to withstand such violence. I expected an arm or a leg to be torn off at any minute!

I finally calmed down enough to recall a parachute free-fall training film I had seen just before my deployment to Vietnam. An image soon became crystal clear in my mind: *Spread eagle to slow down and stabilize.* Any skydiver or figure skater knows this principle, but I was neither. As I responded to the image, which I knew was an answer to the many prayers that had been offered in my behalf, I immediately stopped spinning and tumbling. I was then able to concentrate on other pressing matters—like opening my parachute! If it had opened automatically, I wouldn't have found myself tumbling with such violence.

My mind then cleared further, as if a small TV screen had appeared before me, outlining the rest of the critical emergency procedures I needed to remember. *Check chute.* I didn't have one. *If no chute, pull D-ring.* The D-ring is the rip cord, which I quickly pulled. Immediately the parachute popped out, filled with air, and broke my fall. *Deploy seat kit.* I pulled the lanyard to release the heavy, hard-shelled survival kit that was strapped to my seat. No luck. The kit stayed attached, hanging dangerously behind my thighs.

Later, in my debrief of the ejection, a flight surgeon told me that in every case he knew of, an undeployed seat kit had resulted in a crushed pelvis. I was thankful I was not aware of this grim statistic as I floated toward the earth.

I hadn't realized that Vietnam was in its dry season, and the soft rice field I expected when I landed was concrete hard. I hit my head on the ground and was briefly knocked unconscious. Fortunately I had kept my helmet on throughout the ejection.

When I recovered, I unstrapped myself from my parachute and took a quick inventory. I had no broken bones and saw no enemy troops, but I knew I had landed in hostile territory controlled by the Vietcong. Within thirty minutes a United States Army helicopter arrived, picked me up, and flew me to my intended destination, Soc Trang.

When I finally came down from my adrenalin high and could focus on all that had happened, I became immediately aware of the divine intervention that had occurred in my life. I had experienced major equipment problems: neither the automatic feature on my parachute nor the survival kit release system worked. My spinning had prevented me from thinking clearly until mind-clearing images came to me. And I had landed safely and been rescued from hostile, Vietcong-held territory. In short, it was clear that my prayers and those of my family had been answered in a remarkable fashion.

I know that many soldiers in Vietnam and in other wars who had families praying for them were not so fortunate. I do not know why. I only know that in my case prayer mattered.

Another personal but not so dramatic example of the power of prayer occurred in Leningrad in 1976 at the height of the Cold War. I was serving as the Air Force member of the United States Incidents at Sea negotiating team, and we were on a team tour in the then-Soviet Union. We were guests at a dinner hosted by the commander of the Leningrad Naval District. About fifty senior officers of the navies of the Soviet Union and the United States were present, and the host was leading the group in toasts before dinner. Due to language differences, the proceedings were conducted through interpreters.

We all stood for the first toast and raised our glasses, most of which were filled with the favorite Russian drink, vodka. I had a pink, lemonade-like drink in my glass, which was immediately noticed by the admiral leading the toast. He stopped the proceedings and demanded that I fill my glass with vodka, stating that he would not proceed until I had done so. I declined and told him that I was okay with what I had to drink.

A significant tension began to build when it became evident that he was not going to proceed without my participation. I could sense that even my team members, most of whom were senior to me, were getting somewhat uneasy over the impasse. My Soviet escort, standing at my elbow, hissed in my ear, "Fill your glass with vodka!" In this extremely uncomfortable situation I called on the Lord with the shortest prayer of my life. "God, help me," I pleaded.

Within five seconds, the Soviet interpreter, an army captain with whom I had previously discussed religion, whispered to the host admiral, "It is because of his religion." The admiral nodded his head, the tension immediately diffused, and the program moved on.

I was much relieved to be out of a very embarrassing situation, and it took no great spiritual insight on my part to recognize that the Lord does indeed keep his promises to hear and answer our prayers. In the grand scheme of things, this was not a monumental event, but in my mind it was important to know from my own vivid experience that the Lord will stand squarely behind us when we are trying to hold fast to his standards.

The most dramatic, nonscriptural example of answered prayers that I have ever heard was related to me by Alden Maynes, a Latter-day Saint living in Utah. During World War II, he and his four brothers were called to serve in the armed forces. With her five sons off to war and very much in harm's way, Sister Maynes was deeply concerned for their safety. She went to her bishop, seeking a blessing to help allay her fears. In his blessing, the bishop promised her that through her faith and prayers, her sons would all come home safely. And return safely they did, thanks to obvious divine intervention—most notably in the case of her son Alden.

Alden Maynes was a crew member on a B-17 Flying Fortress stationed in England and flying bombing missions over Germany in the latter part of the war. Germany's intense, well-developed air defenses included fighter aircraft and antiaircraft fire. Consequently, allied losses were high on a majority of the missions—so high that crew members only had to fly twenty-five missions to qualify for rotation back to the United States.

One day in 1944, Brother Maynes was flying with his crew on a mission over Berlin. As usual, the antiaircraft fire was intense, and while the B-17 was flying over the burning city, the enemy shot off its tail. The airplane immediately went out of control, spiraling toward the earth. Inside, it was every crew member for himself as the men scrambled to get out of the tumbling plane through the bomb bay or any other available opening.

The parachutes for crew members on bombers were chest packs that hooked to two D-rings on the parachute harness. The harness was always worn because of the time-consuming effort required to put it on. But the parachute pack itself was cumbersome, so most crewmen kept it handy, hooking it to their chest only when they needed to bail out. That's easily done—unless you lose the tail of your plane and find yourself rocketing to earth inside a crippled aircraft.

Brother Maynes was able to grab his chute and hook one side to his harness. Unfortunately, as he jumped through the escape hatch, the rip cord on his parachute caught on something and opened the chute before he could hook the other side to the harness D-ring. Rather than lower Brother Maynes safely to the ground, his deployed parachute, little more than a single streamer of cord and silk, trailed uselessly above him as he fell toward the burning city below.

Making matters worse, Brother Maynes was well above twenty thousand feet. The air was cold and thin, and he quickly passed out. With bombs falling alongside him, antiaircraft shells exploding around him, a useless parachute streaming above him, and a burning city rushing up to engulf him, Brother Maynes had only a remote chance of surviving. Things didn't look any better when he regained consciousness. But is anything too difficult for the Lord?

As Brother Maynes fell into the city, his seemingly useless, streaming parachute caught on the corner of a building and broke his fall. When he banged against the side of the building, the chute tore loose but then caught on a streetlight. Miraculously, Brother Maynes came to rest, hanging in his harness, with his feet eighteen inches above the ground. He unbuckled his harness and stepped out, with only a racing heart to show for his harrowing experience. He was immediately captured and spent the remainder of the war as a prisoner, but as the bishop promised, he returned home safely, as did his brothers.

I suspect that a hardened cynic could pass off such an amazing survival story as good luck or mere coincidence, but I cannot.

As I listened to Brother Maynes tell his story, I knew he had felt the hand of the Lord in his life on that memorable day, answering his mother's prayers and the bishop's blessing.

One of the most important examples of how the Lord can answer prayers is his appearance to fourteen-year-old Joseph Smith, who desired to know which church to join. Prompted by the admonition, "If any of you lack wisdom, let him ask of God, that giveth to all men liberally, and upbraideth not; and it shall be given him" (James 1:5), Joseph went into the woods to seek direction from the Lord. In answer to his prayer, he received a visitation from God the Father and his Son Jesus Christ. He was instructed to join none of the churches he was considering and was told that he would later participate in the restoration of glorious gospel truths that had been lost during the previous 1800 years.

The life of Joseph Smith is a continuous story of prayers asked and answered. The Prophet's role in translating the Book of Mormon, organizing the Church, and gathering the Saints came in answer to his ongoing prayers. The restoration of gospel truths and principles through him also came as a result of prayer, including the powerful 121st section of the Doctrine and Covenants. The Lord gave this revelation in response to Joseph's prayers in the black depths of Liberty Jail on behalf of the heavily persecuted Saints in Missouri. All Latter-day Saints should be deeply grateful for the productive prayers of the Prophet Joseph Smith.

The young Book of Mormon prophet Nephi was cut out of the same bolt of praying cloth as Joseph Smith. He was led by the Spirit in his quest to secure the brass plates of Laban, he desired to behold the things that his father had seen in his dream of the tree of life, and his faith and prayers were answered with a vision of the life and mission of the Lord Jesus Christ (1 Nephi 4:5–6; 11:1–11, 21–23).

The experience of Enos, son of Jacob, is another uplifting example of answered prayer. Driven by the spiritual admonitions of his father, Enos hungered for relief from his guilt, and he sought the Lord in "mighty prayer and supplication" all day and all night! At the end of this exhausting vigil, he received the relief he sought with the divine words, "Enos, thy sins are forgiven thee, and thou shalt be blessed." Enos recorded the powerful promise of divine response to righteous prayer: "Whatsoever thing ye shall ask in faith, believing that ye shall receive in the name of Christ, ye shall receive it" (Enos 1: 4, 5, 15).

When Adam and Eve were evicted from the Garden of Eden, they "called upon the name of the Lord," built an altar, and prayed for guidance and direction, which they received (Moses 5:4–5). On the banks of the Red Sea, Moses cried unto the Lord. As a result, the sea parted, allowing the fleeing Israelites to escape on dry land (Exodus 14:15–16, 21–22). In Gethsemane, on the eve of the Atonement, Jesus sought his Father's relief and succor in prayer (Matthew 26:39). On the cross the next day, he prayed in a loud voice, "My God, my God, why hast thou forsaken me?" (Matthew 27:46)

Most of the foregoing stories concern life-saving or life-changing events, but prayer should not be reserved for monumental events only. Life's mundane, annoying problems can also be solved through the power of prayer. Don't set your threshold too high for conditions that prompt you to call upon the Lord for help.

A good family example involves my wife and our daughter Kristie. They were driving to Berlin for a brief visit when they became lost in heavy traffic. The map and directions they had been given proved inadequate, it was getting dark, and they were inadvertently heading out of the city toward the Polish border.

"Kristie, do you have your passport with you?" my wife, Gloria, asked.

"Why?" Kristie responded.

"Because we are about to cross the border into Poland," Gloria answered.

"Take the next exit and let's pray," Kristie suggested.

They pulled over, said a prayer, and immediately afterward noticed a taxicab stopped on the side of the road. They pulled alongside the cab and, in Kristie's fair German, communicated their lost condition. The driver led them partway to their destination in Berlin, sending them down the road much relieved. This was not a momentous event, but the Lord responded with immediate assistance to a prayerful plea by two of his daughters facing a dark road in a strange country.

Prayer can play a powerful role in spiritually shaping our lives, especially while we're young. While driving in the mountains of Arizona at the beginning of a short vacation, our son Derek and his wife, Preot, along with their four children, ran into a heavy rainstorm. The storm was so bad that they could hardly see out of the car windshield. When the windshield wipers gave out, they had to pull over. Everyone, especially the children, were eager to get back on the road. After Derek suggested that they offer a prayer to seek the Lord's help, seven-year-old Andrew prayed for the wipers to work or for the rain to stop. Immediately, the wipers hummed into action, and with a cheer of amazement the family resumed their journey.

To reinforce the lesson of the answered prayer, Derek and Preot asked nine-year-old Raile to keep praying for the wipers. When they quit again a few minutes later, Derek asked Raile if she was doing her praying job. She replied that she had forgotten but that she had prayed for them to start again. Her prayer was answered immediately as the wipers started up again.

This sweet story does not end there. Several weeks later while driving with four-year-old Laine, our daughter-in-law mentioned that she was going to the automobile repair shop to get the windshield wipers fixed. Laine asked, "Why, Mom? Why don't you just pray?" She had learned the effectiveness of prayer. Would that we were all so observant regarding how dependable the Lord is in answering our prayers.

Trusting in the Lord with prayers of faith and humility can work wonders in your life. The Lord hears such prayers, and, in his own time and in his own way, he responds—maybe not immediately or in the exact manner you expect, but always in a way most beneficial to you. His perfect love for you will let him do no less.

POINTS TO PONDER

- The Lord's many scriptural promises to answer prayers should give you great confidence and peace of mind.
- This confidence can dramatically increase when you put those promises to the test in your own life.
- The Lord will answer your prayers regarding your smallest problems as well as your biggest challenges.
- To learn to trust the Lord through humble, personal prayers is one of life's most powerful lessons.

CHAPTER 5

Trust in the Word of God

For you shall live by every word that proceedeth forth from the mouth of God. For the word of the Lord is truth (D&C 84:44, 45).

One of the most important factors in developing your ability and willingness to trust in the Lord is to gain confidence and conviction that you can come to know exactly what the Lord expects of you during your life on earth. One of Satan's greatest successes has been his ability to convince most of the Christian world that the heavens are sealed and that there is no need for additional words of divine guidance beyond those found in the Holy Bible. The prophet Nephi saw this satanic success when he recorded, "And because my words shall hiss forth—many of the Gentiles shall say: A Bible! A Bible! We have got a Bible, and there cannot be any more Bible" (2 Nephi 29:3).

We do have a Bible, and it is a glorious book that records critical instructions to the Saints in former days as well as to us in these latter days. But why would we not welcome all of the instructions that the Lord sees fit to give us? Why would the Christian world balk at Joseph Smith's story of a divine visitation in answer to his humble prayer? Does God loves us less than he loved those who received his instructions in biblical times? Are we smarter than the earlier Saints and therefore less in need of additional divine guidance? Is the Bible complete?

No scriptural support exists for the mistaken notion that the Bible is the complete and final word of God. Revelation 22:18, often used to support this notion, states, "If any man shall add unto these things, God shall add unto him the plagues that are written in this book." But John, who wrote the book of Revelation in about 95 A.D., wrote the Gospel of John as well as his epistles *after* he had written Revelation. Besides, the Bible as we know it wasn't even compiled until 1885. So it's easy to deduce that John was referring to the book of Revelation and not to the entire Bible when he wrote that often misused verse.

To further reinforce this observation, we find the same line of thinking written by Moses 1,300 years and 1,331 pages earlier. "Ye shall not add unto the word which I command you, neither shall ye diminish ought from it, that ye may keep the commandments of the Lord your God which I command you" (Deuteronomy 4:2). It does not seem logical that Moses was indicating that all of the books in the Bible following Deuteronomy were wrongfully added.

When we face tough decisions, it's a wonderful feeling to know that we can turn to several scriptural sources for divine instruction. But the word of God also comes to us through the words of living prophets and through inspiration from the Holy Spirit. As Latter-day Saints, we are fortunate that we have definitive doctrine regarding these sources of instruction. This doctrine encourages us to study and use the truths from these three fountains.

TRUST IN THE SCRIPTURES

It is written, man shall not live by bread alone, but by every word that proceedeth out of the mouth of God (Matthew 4:4).

For Latter-day Saints, the scriptures include the King James Version of the Holy Bible; the Book of Mormon, Another Testament of Jesus Christ; the Doctrine and Covenants; and the Pearl of Great Price. These books provide a solid foundation of truth on which we can base our lives. They will have great meaning to us if we will take time to gain a testimony of their divine origin and of their relevance to current challenges and temptations.

The eighth article of faith states, "We believe the Bible to be the word of God as far as it is translated correctly; we also believe the Book of Mormon to be the word of God." A peaceful joy flows over us when we come to an understanding and conviction that we can find valid, life-directing instructions from the Lord if we will but open the scriptures and search their pages for truth and divine wisdom.

Equally joyful is the promise that through spiritual instruction we can come to a firm, personal knowledge of the truthfulness of the eighth article of faith. The promise of Moroni 10:4–5 applies to all truth: "And when ye shall receive these things, I would exhort you that ye would ask God, the Eternal Father, in the name of Christ, if these things are not true; and if ye shall ask with a sincere heart, with real intent, having faith in Christ, he will manifest the truth of it unto you, by the power of the Holy

Ghost. And by the power of the Holy Ghost ye may know the truth of all things."

These instructions have led millions of people to the knowledge that the Book of Mormon is the word of God and, therefore, that Joseph Smith was a true prophet and that the gospel of Jesus Christ has been restored to the earth in these latter days. This knowledge is a treasured possession often called a testimony.

How valuable can the scriptures be in our lives, and how often should we read them? "Priceless," and "regularly, even daily," are good answers to these two important questions. I have a strong testimony of the power of the scriptures to bring special, divine help into our lives.

When I was working in the Pentagon in 1975, I was assigned to a new and very challenging job. I was extremely nervous at the prospect of moving into this assignment because I did not feel prepared to assume the associated responsibilities. I had never been assigned to the area of the world for which I was going to be responsible, and I had never supervised such a large group of extremely talented workers. In short, I was afraid I would fail.

But I was experienced enough to get down on my knees and pray. After praying fervently for several days, I received an answer. One morning the word *scriptures* echoed in my mind. I was confused. What did the scriptures have to do with my new job? The next day I had the same experience, and I realized that I had to pick up the pace of my personal scripture reading. I had read the scriptures all of my life but obviously not with adequate consistency and intensity. I immediately bore down on my daily reading program, with special emphasis on the Book of Mormon.

To this day I cannot explain the connection between the Book of Mormon and my success in that new, challenging job, but I was able to learn the facts, relationships, and staff techniques required to succeed in a dramatically expanded set of responsibilities. I learned to trust in the scriptures!

This type of expanded personal capacity should not surprise us. In an October 1986 general conference address, President Ezra Taft Benson made a promise to members of the Church regarding the unique power found in the Book of Mormon:

"It is not just that the Book of Mormon teaches us truth, though it indeed does that. It is not just that the Book of Mormon bears testimony of Christ, though it indeed does that, too. But there is something more. There is a power in the book which will begin to flow into your lives the moment you begin a serious study of the book. You will find greater power to resist temptation. You will find the power to avoid deception. You will find the power to stay on the straight and narrow path. The scriptures are called 'the words of life' (D&C 84:85), and nowhere is that more true than it is of the Book of Mormon. When you begin to hunger and thirst after those words, you will find life, in greater and greater abundance."[1]

I promise that the more you read the scriptures, the more you will want to read them. I recall as a youth learning that President Harold B. Lee had read the Book of Mormon more than sixty times. You're not in competition with President Lee, but you should be reading the Book of Mormon again and again. It contains a mother lode of truth and inspiration that will strengthen your testimony and enrich your gospel understanding.

Complementing your study of the Book of Mormon with

a study of the Old and New Testaments, the Doctrine and Covenants, and the Pearl of Great Price throughout your life will provide you with knowledge, wisdom, and personal strength that can be found nowhere else. These books truly can provide a solid foundation for your testimony.

TRUST IN THE PROPHETS

Surely the Lord God will do nothing, but he revealeth his secret unto his servants the prophets (Amos 3:7).

On the basis of our testimony of the truths found in the scriptures, we grow eager to know more of the Lord's will regarding our lives. The sixth and ninth articles of faith give us a foundation for faith in modern-day prophets. The sixth article of faith reads, "We believe in the same organization that existed in the Primitive Church, namely, apostles, prophets, pastors, teachers, evangelists, and so forth." The ninth article of faith adds, "We believe all that God has revealed, all that He does now reveal, and we believe that He will yet reveal many great and important things pertaining to the Kingdom of God."

What a blessing it is to know that the Lord calls prophets today and authorizes them to speak for him. Of course, much of the world does not accept the idea of modern-day revelation. But why would our Father in Heaven, who loves us and wants to lead us back into his presence, not give us the same level of personal guidance and instruction that he gave to his children in biblical times?

We are certainly no more intelligent or spiritual than were the Saints two thousand years ago. In fact, we face threats today that are not even covered in ancient scripture. Drugs, pornography, and attacks on the family are but a few of the challenges that modern prophets must address. Fortunately, youth of The Church of Jesus Christ of Latter-day Saints can turn to the prophet for guidance on these and many other important issues of our time.

I can testify with conviction that I know that Gordon B. Hinckley is the Lord's chosen prophet on the earth today. The Holy Spirit has born this testimony to me in a powerful way. In April 1995, during the first session of general conference, a session that had been designated as a solemn assembly, Church members around the world had the opportunity to sustain President Hinckley as the new prophet.

My wife and I were living in McLean, Virginia, at the time and were sitting in our home watching conference on television. President Hinckley was conducting the session and was standing at the pulpit making his opening remarks. I was leaning forward listening, when suddenly the Holy Spirit flooded over me. My eyes filled with tears, and I could not speak. The Spirit had testified to me that President Hinckley was indeed the Lord's prophet on the earth. I turned to explain to my wife what had happened to me and could see that the same thing had happened to her.

Since then, I have been impressed by President Hinckley's spiritual instruction, broad-ranging activities, and seemingly limitless energy. They all testify that the Lord sustains him in his calling, both spiritually and physically. But beyond all of this, I know that he is the Lord's prophet because of a personal, unsolicited witness from the Holy Ghost. I am so thankful for a prophet on the earth today and for the inspired instruction he gives to all who will listen.

One of our sons had a similar experience while he was attending Brigham Young University. President Spencer W. Kimball was to address the student body, and our son Perry was among twenty thousand noisy students awaiting the prophet's arrival. As Perry scanned the crowd looking for a friend, an overpowering feeling came over him and the rest of the student body. He felt as if he was on fire. When Perry looked toward the rostrum area, he saw that President Kimball had entered the hall. The Spirit was strong, testifying that Spencer W. Kimball was indeed the prophet of the Lord.

President Hinckley's oft-repeated advice to believe in Jesus Christ and in his atonement, to strengthen our families, to keep the Sabbath day holy, to retain new converts, to be clean, to avoid pornography, and to pay an honest tithe has special relevance for youth and adults alike in our world today. President Hinckley's dynamic leadership in the building of temples across the face of the earth and his strong encouragement of members to attend the temple are special hallmarks of his tenure as prophet. His counsel can become a solid foundation for those with ears to hear.

Of particular value to young men and young women today is President Hinckley's counsel on "ways to be." He has advised young people to be grateful, smart, involved, clean, true, positive, humble, still, and prayerful.[2] Each of these important attributes has slipped in value in today's world. Consequently, it is appropriate and even predictable that God's prophet would give young men and young women timely, powerful counsel to help them align their lives with the Lord's will.

May we all have the courage throughout our lives to listen closely to the Lord's prophet and to trust his inspired counsel.

TRUST IN THE SPIRIT

For behold, again I say unto you that if ye will enter in by the way, and receive the Holy Ghost, it will show unto you all things what ye should do (2 Nephi 32:5).

Despite the power and clarity of the scriptures and the admonitions of living prophets, the most valuable source of divine guidance in your life should be the influence of the Holy Ghost. Because you have been baptized and confirmed a member of the Church, you have the right to receive personalized promptings through the gift of the Holy Ghost.

These promptings can address events across the entire spectrum of your life: personal and family safety, finances, interpersonal relationships, professional decisions, and so forth. And they can come to you in many different forms: a still small voice, an audible voice, an inspired thought, a dream, a strong feeling or impression, a spiritual response to a church hymn, or even a vision. Whatever the medium, the message is personal and divinely designed to help you through trials or tests or to aid you in making major decisions. You increase your sensitivity to the promptings of the Holy Ghost every time you heed his instructions, even to the point that the Holy Ghost can become your constant companion.

By virtue of their calling, prophets in every age have had access to the promptings of the Holy Spirit. But the workings of the Spirit aren't limited to prophets; they're available to all of God's children who humble and prepare themselves to be guided from on high. A few personal examples may help you understand how the Spirit can guide you in making correct decisions.

My wife, Gloria, tells a special, personal story of her youth that graphically illustrates the great blessings available to those who listen to the promptings of the Spirit. As a young girl, she lived in Chicago with her family. After her father died when she was twelve, her mother decided to move to Utah, where she had been offered a job. As Gloria, her mother, and two sisters were driving on a winding, dangerous stretch of highway in central Utah on their way to BYU, her mother heard a voice say, "Slow down." She continued on at the same speed, and then she heard the voice a second time repeat the words, "Slow down." This time she obeyed. Moments later, a large coal truck came barreling around a corner on the wrong side of the road, just a short distance in front of them. It is obvious what would have happened had Gloria's mother not heeded the Spirit's promptings and slowed down.

This incident is somewhat unusual because the result, had Gloria's mother not heeded the prompting, became readily apparent. We must be willing to heed promptings even if we don't immediately perceive a physical or spiritual threat.

Several years ago, just before our son Bart married, we were discussing the upcoming festivities. It was early in the evening, and it was raining heavily outside. Suddenly the groom-to-be declared that he and a friend were going for a drive to check out the mountain cabin that had been selected for the honeymoon. I felt that the drive was not a good idea, but Bart reaffirmed his intention to go. A feeling of gloom came over me, and I left the room. My wife soon followed me and indicated that she too had a dark feeling about the proposed trip.

We called Bart out of the living room and told him of our feelings. He went off by himself and pondered our words. He shortly returned and stated, "Well, I don't feel anything bad will happen, but you are my parents, and if you have those feelings, I will respect them and not go." Relief flooded over us at his response. Because he didn't go, we never learned what mishap might have occurred, but there is no doubt in our minds that it was something that could have halted the upcoming temple marriage. That obedient, trusting son is now a bishop with five young children. He has continued to trust in the Spirit with regards to his family, Church, and professional activities.

As a young man or young woman, you also need to develop sufficient spiritual sensitivity so that you can hear, understand, and heed the voice of the Spirit. By following the Spirit, you demonstrate your faith and trust in the Lord, which makes him more willing to bless you with additional promptings.

Heaven-sent promptings can help us with such small things as locating lost car keys and with such significant things as saving our lives. They can also direct us to life-changing events or relationships.

Our oldest son, Perry, and his wife, Marci, have always been close to the Spirit. Unable to have biological children, they adopted two wonderful children. Because they desired a larger family, they began looking for another child to adopt. During this same period, they moved across the country to a new Air Force assignment and began looking for a home to buy. They found several nice homes but didn't feel right about any of them after praying for help in making their choice. They then looked at lots with the intent of building a home, settling on one lot that looked much like others they had considered. Their choice was confirmed through prayer, but they had no idea at the time what was special about their chosen lot's location.

A few months after moving into their newly built home, Marci took her four-year-old daughter to play with a neighbor girl she had met at church. As Marci visited with the little girl's mother, they discussed adoption and Marci and Perry's longing and prayers for another child. The neighbor confided that her unwed sister was expecting a baby in the near future and was looking for a home for the child. Today that child is a much-loved and vital part of our son's family. There is no question that the Spirit was interested in where our son and his family lived.

I can testify that the Spirit directly manages many of the affairs of the Church, including general conference. When I was called to the Seventy in April 2000, I knew that I would be asked to give a short conference talk in the new Conference Center. I was nervous at the prospect of speaking before twenty-two thousand assembled Saints plus millions more who would be listening around the world, but I started to mentally prepare my talk anyway.

A few months later, in late August, I was advised that I would have the opportunity to speak during general conference in October. I immediately sat down and started to write the talk that by then was fairly well developed in my mind. The first paragraph flowed as planned, but the second paragraph seemed to have a mind of its own. I was soon off on an entirely different track than I had expected, writing down thoughts on various aspects of missionary work.

At the end of the day, my rough draft no longer contained my now irrelevant first paragraph. Early the next morning, I awoke with a missionary story on my mind about a host failing to offer a glass of freshly squeezed orange juice to a breakfast guest. When the guest asked the host why he had withheld the juice, the host replied, "I was afraid you might not like orange juice, and I didn't want to offend you by offering you something you didn't desire."[3] The obvious message was that we are often reluctant to share the gospel with our friends for fear of offending them. I knew immediately that this story had not come from my mind, and I included it in my nearly finished conference talk.

By the end of the next day, I had completed my talk. It lacked only the finishing polish. I had previously wondered how the conference talks always seemed to fit together so well, with little overlap. On the basis of my personal experience, I learned that the Spirit will fill the role of coordinator if the speakers will simply listen and trust.

POINTS TO PONDER

- Your Father in Heaven wants you to return to his presence to dwell with him eternally. He has provided a return path for you called the plan of salvation or the plan of happiness.

- This marvelous plan, with all of its supporting details and instructions, has come to us through divine revelation. Revelation comes to us through the written word in the scriptures, the spoken word of modern prophets, and the personal, sweet instructions of the Holy Ghost.

- The more we seek and trust God's word, the more we will hunger for his light and direction in our lives.

NOTES

1. Ezra Taft Benson, "The Book of Mormon: Keystone of Our Religion," *Ensign,* October 1986, 34–35.
2. Gordon B. Hinckley, *Way to Be* (New York: Simon & Schuster, 2002), 11.
3. Robert C. Oaks, "Sharing the Gospel," *Ensign,* November 2000, 81.

CHAPTER 6

Trust When You Cannot See

And it came to pass that I, Nephi, said unto my father: I will go and do the things which the Lord hath commanded, for I know that the Lord giveth no commandments unto the children of men, save he shall prepare a way for them that they may accomplish the thing which he commandeth them (1 Nephi 3:7).

*B*lind obedience is an unappealing term with a mindless, unthinking undertone. The Lord, rather than demand that you obey him blindly, wants you to come to a position of knowledge and understanding through trust, obedience, and faith.

The laws of God are vast and complex. If you delay obedience to his laws until you understand all of their ramifications, you will never take even the first step in aligning your life with his will. But if you show trust and faith through obedience, God will instruct you as needed so that you can take your first faltering steps toward him. He will richly reward those shaky steps, providing you with a foundation for your trust and faith, and he will confirm in your heart through the Holy Ghost that those meager steps are conducive to your spiritual growth and eternal joy. This trust and faith will help you move forward with confidence even though you cannot see the end of your journey or understand all of the pitfalls and stumbling blocks in your path. Eventually, you will realize that no matter how big the obstacle or steep the grade, the Lord will be there to help you.

The process of moving through life by faith is beautifully depicted in Lehi's vision of the murky mist and the iron rod. Likewise, you cannot see the end goal clearly, but you can trust in the iron rod—the word of God—and navigate your way through the fogs and dangerous distractions of life.

I still recall the first rule of instrument flying from my days in pilot training. When you're piloting an aircraft in the clear, cloudless air, you rely on your physical senses of seeing and feeling to maintain your equilibrium and to know which way is up, which way you're turning, and which way you're heading. You keep oriented by simply looking through the windscreen. But after you enter the clouds, your physical senses can easily fool you. With the loss of a visual horizon, gradual turns or turbulence can cause vertigo, which can quickly render you incapable of maintaining control of your aircraft. Hundreds of airplanes and thousands of lives have been lost because pilots have become disoriented while flying in the clouds, unable to see the horizon or their final destination.

Your equilibrium is closely tied to your inner ear and your eyesight. When you have no visual reference, your inner ears can convince you that you are turning when you are actually flying straight and level or that you are flying straight and level when you are, in fact, turning.

The problem is complex, but the solution is simple. The first and most important rule for flying in cloudy weather is to trust your instruments. Believe and follow their indications even though your physical senses shout something different in your ears.

Modern aircraft are equipped with instruments that tell speed, direction, altitude, and *attitude*. In flying vernacular, *attitude* means the aircraft's orientation to the horizon or to the earth's surface—whether you're upside down or right side up, banking or turning, climbing or diving. The attitude indicator is simply a gyroscopically driven artificial horizon, but it's your most important instrument for flying aircraft safely in clouds or darkness.

Invariably, in the clouds your senses will be fooled and let you down—maybe way down. The only safe course is to trust your instruments. On several occasions while I was flying in clouds or at night, my inner ears nearly overwhelmed my judgment, telling me that I was in a steep turn, when I was actually flying straight and level. In every case, if I had not trusted my instruments completely, I would have made wrong, unnecessary corrections, with probable disastrous results.

In my flying career, the assignment that demanded the most trust and discipline came in 1970 when I was assigned to Nellis Air Force Base near Las Vegas to begin training in the F-111 fighter. The F-111 was a deep-penetration aircraft, best used at night or in bad weather. It was equipped with terrain-following radar (TFR), which let it hug the ground even when you couldn't see anything outside the cockpit. It also had a sophisticated attack radar, which would let you find small, well-hidden targets while you were flying very low (two hundred feet above the ground) and very fast (1.2 Mach at low altitude or 2.2 Mach at high altitude) in the dark. The F-111 represented the most advanced technology when it first flew in 1963.

I realized the great need for trust in technology on my first nighttime TFR training mission. Taking off at dusk from Nellis, we flew out over the desert. By the time we got to the letdown area where we would begin our low-level training, it was dark, but we could still see a dim horizon. To fly safely at low levels, we needed to put the aircraft on autopilot and take our hands off the aircraft control stick. We would only move the throttle to make sure that we had enough speed to clear mountain peaks and to stay on schedule with our flight plan. We watched the TFR scope closely to make sure it worked properly. But the reality was that for some failures, we would have had little time to react. We simply had to trust the system. If we didn't, we couldn't relax enough to complete the tasks required of the pilot and the navigator.

No F-111 crew member could relax on that first TFR training flight. Nor could we relax on the second night flight or on the third. But as we saw the system operate time after time as it was designed, and as we became more competent in performing our duties, we began to calm down. Some pilots and navigators even got to the point that they enjoyed these night flights. But enjoy them or not, everyone had to learn to trust the TFR system, as well as all of the other aircraft systems.

Flying low level at night or in the clouds is similar to living happily on earth. In both endeavors success depends on your willingness to trust. In flying, you must trust your instruments and aircraft systems to give you accurate information and let you understand the big picture. To enjoy a happy life, it is equally important to trust the Lord. Because of his love and knowledge, he will provide you with accurate information and direction that will let you understand the bigger, eternal picture.

It is so easy and natural to trust your physical senses, desires, and appetites, rationalizing that they are in good working order and giving you proper direction. But like your inner ear, they can give you impressions, vectors, and attitudes that may take you to unhappy destinations. At such times, you desperately need heading and attitude indications from the Lord. You need to seek him out and trust his counsel and directions.

Trust is also required if we are to learn the lessons we need to learn and accomplish the things we need to accomplish in our short lifetime. Flying safely is a matter of discipline, and nowhere is your discipline more challenged than in overcoming your natural desire to trust your physical senses, even though you know they can be wrong. You must discipline yourself and trust the instruments God has provided to help you stay on course.

Just as there is little chance of physical survival if you crash in a high-speed jet fighter, you stand little chance of spiritual survival if you repeatedly crash yourself against God's laws. True, you can repent, put the pieces of your life back together, and get back on course at a safe altitude, but it is much better to stay away from the rough terrain that awaits the errant, untrusting soul. Just as I learned to trust the engineers who had designed the F-111 and the mechanics who maintained it, so must you learn to trust our all-knowing Lord, who has lovingly provided us with rules for a happy, productive journey through life.

If we pay attention to how the Lord keeps his promises, we will be led to an attitude of faith and trust. When we note how our prayers are answered, our obedience is rewarded, and our faithful lives are blessed, how can we not trust the lawgiver and his words? He has given us a sure navigation system in this life called the gospel of Jesus Christ. The only failure that occurs in his system is operator error.

The scriptures are filled with counsel and commandments instructing us to trust in the arm of the Lord. Let's consider a few of these scriptures as well as some personal experiences, looking for specific ways in which we can focus our trust and paying special attention to the promised blessings that come to those who trust in the Lord throughout their lives.

One of the greatest scriptural examples of faith and trust in the Lord is that of the Book of Mormon prophet Nephi. This young man showed great courage and trust when his father asked him and his three older brothers—Laman, Lemuel, and Sam—to return to Jerusalem to secure the brass plates.

"And it came to pass that I, Nephi, said unto my father: I will go and do the things which the Lord hath commanded, for I know that the Lord giveth no commandments unto the children of men, save he shall prepare a way for them that they may accomplish the thing which he commandeth them" (1 Nephi 3:7).

The brass plates were held by Laban, a strong and powerful Israelite leader who accused Laman of being a robber when he sought to obtain the records. After Laman had fled from Laban, he and Lemuel wanted to give up on their divinely directed mission. But with another powerful expression of faith that showed trust and courage far beyond his years, Nephi convinced his brothers to return to Jerusalem.

"But behold I said unto them that: As the Lord liveth, and as we live, we will not go down unto our father in the wilderness until we have accomplished the thing which the Lord hath commanded us" (1 Nephi 3:15).

The brothers returned to their abandoned home to collect their family riches, hoping to trade them for the plates. But Laban confiscated their riches and then sought to kill them. After they had fled to safety, Laman and Lemuel renewed their murmuring and harassment of Nephi, striking him and Sam with a rod. But with assistance from an angel, Nephi convinced his brothers to return to Jerusalem one last time and to seek a way to secure the treasured plates of brass. Nephi had no plan, only his faith that the Lord would provide a way. He summed up his faith and trust with a brief but powerful statement: "And I was led by the Spirit, not knowing beforehand the things which I should do" (1 Nephi 3:28–29; 4:6).

Upon returning to the city, Nephi found Laban on the ground near his house, drunk. Nephi was constrained by the Spirit to slay Laban, but the thought repulsed him. The Spirit then said to him, "Behold the Lord slayeth the wicked to bring forth his righteous purposes. It is better that one man should perish than that a nation should dwindle and perish in unbelief" (1 Nephi 4:13).

Because of his faith and trust in the Lord, Nephi did as he was commanded. Then, using Laban's armor and clothing as a disguise, Nephi proceeded to Laban's house and obtained the brass plates as his father had directed.

Nephi likely did not understand the key role these plates would play in the spiritual development and preservation of his people during the next one thousand years. He only knew that his father, a prophet of the Lord, had instructed him to secure the plates so that his family might take them on their journey. Nephi provided the trust; the Lord provided the way.

A powerful but less familiar story of trusting in the Lord and in things we cannot see is that of Elisha. As recorded in the Old Testament, the prophet Elisha, on more than one occasion, had provided the king of Israel with valuable intelligence about the intentions of the Syrian army to lay ambushes for the army of Israel. The king of Syria, desiring to eliminate this effective Israelite source of intelligence, surrounded Dothan, the city where Elisha resided.

When Elisha's servant saw the formidable hosts all about, he despaired and cried, "Alas, my master! How shall we do? And he [Elisha] answered, Fear not: for they that be with us are more than they that be with them." Elisha's trust and faith in the Lord allowed the servant to see that "the mountain was full of horses and chariots of fire round about Elisha." Elisha then prayed that the enemy would be blinded, after which he led them away to Samaria (2 Kings 6:15–19).

You too can develop trust and faith in the Lord that will lead you to understand the great truth that even though you cannot see, you should not fear. "They that be with [you]," after all, "are more than they that be with them." Despite the persistence and cleverness of Satan, the forces of heaven are more numerous and more powerful. These forces are on call to serve those who put their trust in the Lord.

POINTS TO PONDER

- A prime goal and purpose of your mortal life on earth is to grow in faith and trust.

- You grow in faith by hearing the word of God, testing it by obeying its precepts, and observing promised blessings in your life and in the lives of those around you.
- Hold firmly to the iron rod, the word of God, so you can make your way along gospel paths.

CHAPTER 7

Trust in the Lord through Obedience

And now, verily, verily, I say unto thee, put your trust in that Spirit which leadeth to do good—yea, to do justly, to walk humbly, to judge righteously; and this is my Spirit (D&C 11:12).

The surest way to demonstrate your trust and faith in the strength and power of the Lord is through your obedience to his laws and commandments. The Soviet Union had a saying to describe its large but relatively unsophisticated military force: "Quantity has a quality of its own." In the context of a discussion on obedience, we might say, "Obedience has a virtue of its own."

The Lord keeps his promises through a cycle of obedience and blessings. When we experience that cycle in our lives, our faith and trust in the Lord grow. In turn, our faith and trust provide a foundation for our increased determination to obey.

As a young man in my early twenties, I had an experience that left me with a deep appreciation for the powerful virtue that is associated with obedience. I had let myself become distracted from gospel growth by worrying about how prehistoric animals fit into the biblical recounting of the origins of life. I had a strong testimony of the Joseph Smith story and of the divine origins of the Book of Mormon, but I could not get past my prehistoric hang-up.

I found myself not wanting to go to Church until I could solve my dilemma, but I decided one day that I knew by the power of the Holy Spirit that the gospel was true and that I had best not jeopardize that knowledge by too much attention to things I did not understand. Through these disturbing months, I kept going to Church and fulfilling the duties of my various callings. And then the virtue of obedience manifested itself in my life. As a result, my doubts just went away. I became satisfied that when I needed to know those other things, I would have access to the necessary information. Since that time, I have spent zero energy on what seemed so important for a short period.

The scriptures are filled with examples of those who demonstrated their trust in the Lord through their obedience. From Adam to Jesus Christ, those who did the work of the Lord listened to and obeyed his word, while those who refused to listen and obey hindered his work.

After they were expelled from the Garden of Eden, Adam and Eve sought direction from the Lord. They were obedient to the direction and commandments they received, and Adam led his children in righteousness (Moses 5:4–5).

Because of the gross wickedness of the people in his day, Noah was instructed by the Lord to build an ark and gather animals. He obeyed, despite the jeers and ridicule of everyone about him. Through his faith and obedience, Noah and his family were saved from the Flood (Genesis 7:23).

Abraham was directed and blessed by the Lord throughout his life because of his obedient heart. His promised blessings extend far beyond this mortal life. By following heavenly direction, Abraham led his family, through Isaac and Jacob, into a remarkable series of covenants with the Lord that would yield eternal blessings to his family and to all righteous men and women who would hearken unto the Lord (Genesis 12–25).

Through his obedience to the laws of God and by listening closely to the Lord's counsel, Jacob's son Joseph rose to a position of great influence in Pharaoh's court. From this position, he was able to save his family from starvation in time of drought. When his brothers came from the land of Canaan seeking food and relief, they found an obedient, forgiving brother whom they had sold into slavery several years before (Genesis 37–50).

Four hundred years later, Moses heard and heeded the voice of the Lord, leaving a life of palatial luxury and leading his people out of Egyptian slavery (Exodus 2–15).

Samuel hearkened to the Lord all of his days and was thus able to provide prophetic guidance, first to King Saul and then to David. Samuel was the Lord's agent in selecting and anointing David as a youth (1 Samuel 3–16).

Saul, on the other hand, had trouble hearkening to the Lord. Saul had been instructed to take his army and destroy the Amalekites, a people who had harassed the Israelites as they came from Egypt to the land of Canaan. He was also commanded to destroy the Amalekites' livestock. Saul almost obeyed. He killed most of the people and most of the animals but saved the Amalekite king and "the best of the sheep, and of the oxen, and of the fatlings, and the lambs, and all that was good" (1 Samuel 15:9).

By his disobedience, Saul elevated his judgment above the Lord's, which is usually what happens when we disobey.

When he approached the prophet Samuel, Saul lied, saying, "I have performed the commandment of the Lord." Samuel replied, "What meaneth then this bleating of the sheep in mine ears, and the lowing of the oxen which I hear?" Saul's feeble excuse that he intended to sacrifice the animals to the Lord impressed neither Samuel nor the Lord. Samuel rejected Saul's pleas, closing with a great statement on strict obedience to divine instructions: "Behold, to obey is better than sacrifice, and to hearken than the fat of rams." As a consequence of his disobedience, Saul soon found himself without the support of the Lord and eventually without a kingdom (1 Samuel 15:13, 14, 22, 23, 26).

Few stories better illustrate the relationship of humility and obedience than the story of Naaman, captain of the Syrian army. Afflicted with leprosy, he was counseled to go to the prophet Elisha to be healed. But when Naaman came to the door, Elisha sent word for him to "go and wash in Jordan seven times, and thy flesh shall come again to thee, and thou shalt be clean" (2 Kings 5:10). This was not what Naaman had expected of a prophet, and he departed in a rage.

Fortunately, Naaman was blessed with a wise and courageous servant who counseled him, "My father, if the prophet had bid thee do some great thing, wouldest thou not have done it? How much rather then, when he saith to thee, Wash, and be clean?" This mighty soldier then humbled himself and did as he had been instructed. "Then went he down, and dipped himself seven times in Jordan, according to the saying of the man of God: and his flesh came again like unto the flesh of a little child, and he was clean" (2 Kings 5:13–14).

The mightiest of all prophets, Jesus Christ, prophesied much about the future of those who would follow him or reject him. He taught basic, eternal laws that we must obey if we wish to return to his presence, and he reminded his disciples that everything he did was directed by the Father. His life became a pattern for charity and service but especially for obedience.

The Book of Mormon also teaches lessons on obedience. Under the direction of a long line of prophets, Book of Mormon people were led in paths of righteousness, but they repeatedly left those paths to follow Satan. Not surprisingly, they repeatedly paid a high price for their failure to heed the words of the prophets.

Abinadi stood before the priests of wicked King Noah and declared words of faith and repentance that the Lord had instructed him to give. Abinadi's words fell primarily on deaf ears, he died a martyr's death, and the people suffered for failing to follow his counsel (Mosiah 11–17).

Nearly 150 years later, Samuel the Lamanite offered the wicked Nephites the same opportunity to repent, follow the Lord's eternal laws, and avoid destruction. But many of them were caught up in the ways of the world and rejected Samuel's words (Helaman 13–16).

Following his resurrection, Christ appeared to the Book of Mormon people and established his Church among them. They lived in obedience and peace for two hundred years but then reverted to wickedness. Within two centuries, they had secured their destruction by ignoring the Lord's guidance and counsel.

For the better part of two thousand years following the death of Jesus Christ, the prophets were silenced by the darkness and depth of the Great Apostasy. The imaginations of the people were captured by the philosophies of men rather than by the pronouncements of the Lord through his prophets. Truly, the darkness of the Dark Ages had settled upon the minds of God's children.

In 1820, in response to a simple prayer, God opened the heavens once again and gave divine instructions to a young prophet. From that day until his death, Joseph Smith received a nearly continual stream of heavenly directions as he played out his foreordained tasks in the restoration of the gospel of Jesus Christ. Joseph heard and heeded, dedicating his entire life to the building up of the kingdom of God on earth.

Obedience is not always easy. It demands that you humble yourself and acknowledge that someone knows more than you and that there is a better path to follow than the one you might blaze for yourself. By obedience to God's instructions, we can take full advantage of his limitless vision and boundless love and thereby avoid many of life's inevitable pitfalls. When we are on the Lord's path, we cannot go astray.

Elder Russell M. Nelson's willingness to obey the instructions of the Lord's latter-day prophets, even before his call to the Quorum of the Twelve Apostles, illustrates this point. While serving as general president of the Sunday School, Elder Nelson attended a 1979 regional representatives' seminar at which President Spencer W. Kimball challenged those in attendance to lengthen their stride in spreading the gospel.

"We should be of service to the Chinese," President Kimball

said. "We should learn their language. We should pray for them and help them."[1]

Elder Nelson returned home from that meeting and told his wife, Dantzel, that they needed to get some books and hire a tutor so that they could start learning Mandarin, which they did reasonably well. The far-reaching effects of Elder Nelson's obedience were dramatically demonstrated sometime later at the annual meetings of the American Association of Thoracic Surgery.

While taking notes during a presentation, Elder Nelson felt impressed to initiate a conversation in Mandarin with a distinguished Chinese surgeon. From that conversation, a friendship developed that eventually allowed Elder Nelson to share his surgical expertise with the people of mainland China and in the process generate a tremendous amount of goodwill. Great blessings resulted because Elder Nelson had the courage, humility, and determination to trust and obey the prophet's voice.[2]

Unless you're called to serve a mission in China, it's unlikely that you will ever be asked to learn Mandarin. It's even less likely that you will ever be called upon to build an ark. But you *are* called upon to live the law of chastity, the law of tithing, the Word of Wisdom, and many other laws of the gospel of Jesus Christ, all of which are founded on eternal truths. Obeying these laws is much easier when you come to trust them as foundation stones for a rich, rewarding, and righteous life.

POINTS TO PONDER

- Trust, obedience, blessings, and faith are part of an upward spiritual spiral. You learn about a commandment of the Lord and trust him enough to obey it. You enjoy resultant blessings and grow in your faith. You learn about a more difficult command-ment, and with your increased faith you trust enough to obey and are blessed again for your obedience. You again grow in faith, and the cycle repeats itself.

NOTES

1. Spencer W. Condie, *Russell M. Nelson: Father, Surgeon, Apostle* (Salt Lake City: Deseret Book, 2003), 215.
2. Ibid., 216.

*I didn't make the BYU freshman football team, but a year later, in 1955,
I got to run BYU plays the week our Air Force Academy Hamburger Squad
prepared to play the Cougars.*

*My father, Charles Oaks, was a
great BYU football player in 1935.*

Throughout all of my young life, my mother, Ann Oaks, was my strongest supporter.

I will be forever grateful for the love and instruction my parents gave me.

FIRST CLASS AT THE U. S. AIR FORCE ACADEMY: Just nine hours after reporting the first class to enter the new U. S. Air Force Academy stands at attention, about to be sworn in en masse at Lowry Air Force Base near Denver, Colo.

USAFA - As The First Class Arrived

As members of the first class of the new Air Force Academy, we had to quickly learn to march and stand at attention for opening-day festivities.

I graduated from the Air Force Academy in 1959 as a second lieutenant.

I was flying a Lockheed T-33 Shooting Star like this one when instructors thought they might have to shoot me down during a disastrous pilot-training check ride.

To fly this close at low altitude, you must trust both your leader and your wingman. This flight of ten F-100 Super Sabers is soaring two hundred feet over a target in a firepower demonstration at Nellis Air Force Base, near Las Vegas, Nevada, in 1962. I'm flying the third aircraft up from the lower right.

My 1964 audition flight for the United States Air Force Aerial Demonstration Team, the Thunderbirds, was no more successful than my tryout for the BYU freshman football team. But at least I wasn't sore after practice.

In 1965, the 416th Tactical Fighter Squadron departed for Vietnam. I'm the fourth pilot from the right in the back row.

In Vietnam we often had the opportunity to fly visiting dignitaries. Here I am debriefing the Air Force Academy commandant of cadets, Brig. Gen. Louis Seith, following an F-100 combat mission.

I was flying an F-100 Super Saber like this one when I was shot down over Vietnam on March 30, 1966. It was a day when prayer mattered.

As commander of the 391st Tactical Fighter Squadron, I regularly flew the F-111 swingwing fighter.

The complexity of the F-111 swingwing fighter, as with most modern aircraft, demands the trust and confidence of the pilot and crew.

Strapped in the cockpit of my fighter, I'm getting ready to fly a training mission in Germany.

I was able to fly the F-16 Viper throughout my tour as commander of the United States Air Force in Europe. In flying formation, you must keep your eyes focused on your leader and trust him to lead you safely to your destination.

Reporter Mike Wallace trusted my report and decided not to do the negative story about German-American relations he had planned.

Whether you're flying World War II vintage C-47s or the up-to-date B-1, trusting in the performance of others is a central part of aviation. You must rely on the work of designers, engineers, mechanics, and controllers.

Provide Promise

April 6, 1993 -- General Oaks flies a Provide Promise airdrop mission to Bosnia. (Combat Camera Imagery).

In 1993 I was privileged to fly on some satisfying night-drop missions in the C-130, carrying supplies to refugees in Bosnia.

This is my official Air Force photo taken at the time of my promotion to four-star rank in 1990.

In keeping with Air Force tradition, Brock and Gloria hose me down after my final flight in an F-16 at Ramstein Air Base in Germany. Afterward, I gave Gloria a wet bear hug.

I review the troops at the conclusion of a change-of-command ceremony just before my retirement from the United States Air Force in 1994. Little did I realize that four days later I would lie unconscious in a hospital in Virginia.

A KC-135 Tanker (top) prepares to refuel a C-141 transport aircraft. On my last opportunity to pilot an Air Force aircraft, I flew home from Germany with Gloria in a C-141, which we refueled over the North Atlantic.

Here's our family in a picture taken following my retirement after thirty-five years of service in the United States Air Force (from left): Capt. Perry Oaks, 2d Lt. Brock Oaks, Keri Oaks, Gen. Robert C. Oaks, Gloria Oaks, Kristie Oaks, 1st Lt. Derek Oaks, and Capt. Bart Oaks.

Here are our grandchildren of windshield wiper trust and fame (from left): Rail, Andrew, Laine, and Emma.

I enjoyed meeting the children of the newly formed Marameu Branch in East Central Mozambique. The branch chapel is behind us.

During our three years in Southeast Africa, we saw the Church grow rapidly because of the people's firm faith. Here we are breaking ground for the Bedfordview chapel in Johannesburg, South Africa.

On a mission tour while serving as Africa Southeast Area president with my wife, Gloria, I had the opportunity to meet with the hardworking missionaries in Mutare, Zimbabwe.

CHAPTER 8

Trust in the Law of Chastity

For I, the Lord God, delight in the chastity of women. And whore-doms are an abomination before me; thus saith the Lord of Hosts (Jacob 2:28).

Many words have been directed toward the youth of the Church regarding the importance of living the Lord's law of sexual morality, known as the law of chastity. But with all of the satanic influences, subtle and direct, assaulting young people today, it seems unnecessary to apologize for speaking about this important subject one more time. The costs of mistakes with respect to the law of chastity are high and eternal. Repentance for violating this law is possible but difficult. An ounce of prevention is worth much more than a pound of cure.

Immoral behavior, including necking, petting, and all forms of illicit sexual relations, are encouraged by many elements of modern society. Movies, television programs, websites, rock and rap music, and school friends can all be sources of encouragement for relaxing time-proven standards embodied in the law of chastity. Given the strength of physical attraction between young men and young women, it doesn't take a lot of encouragement to persuade some young people to rush beyond the bounds the Lord has outlined.

The results of violating the law of chastity are not always readily apparent. Every experimenting young girl does not get pregnant. Every experimenting young man does not acquire a sexually transmitted disease. These results are threatening and devastating but not universal. What is universal for those who disregard the warning flags waved by concerned parents, bishops, and youth advisers is the loss of self-respect, spiritual sensitivity, and good standing in the Church.

Thanks to the scriptures and modern-day prophets, you have a clear picture of exactly what the Lord expects. You do not have to subject yourself to the pain and punishment associated with violating this law in order to realize that the Lord's way is the right way. Society's relaxed standards are just more of Satan's traps that draw you in with the cleverly disguised bait of early dating, late nights alone, and physical intimacy.

The scriptures are an excellent source for building trust in the wisdom of the Lord and developing discipline and restraint. His instructions regarding sexual sin start with the Ten Commandments in the Old Testament (Exodus 20:14) and continue through all recorded scripture, including the Doctrine and Covenants (132:41–44). Throughout the scriptures, fornication, adultery, and "anything like unto it" (D&C 59:6) all lead to the same painful, unhappy end.

King David's fall as a result of sexual misconduct must certainly stand as one of the Bible's most tragic events. Despite the many times you have studied this story, its warning remains instructive today.

David tarried in Jerusalem while his army was in the field, laying siege to the city of Rabbah. "Tarried" as used here means that he wasn't where he should have been, which was with his armies. As he tarried, he looked out over the city and saw Bathsheba bathing on a nearby rooftop (2 Samuel 11:1–2).

Any well instructed deacon knows that when you happen to see something you shouldn't see, you need to close your eyes, turn your head, and remove yourself from the temptation. David obviously missed that lesson because he hung around and "enquired after the woman." Worse yet, when he found out that she was Uriah's wife, warning bells should have gone off in his head. But by sending for Bathsheba, he put himself in such a compromising situation that he must have decided that the law of chastity no longer applied to him (2 Samuel 11:3).

As a result of David's adultery, Bathsheba conceived and David was driven into a series of lies and deceits that eventually led him to arrange for Uriah's death in battle. David's fall can be blamed directly on his failure to heed several obvious danger signs. He was aroused by the sight of a woman washing herself. He allowed his interest in her to increase to the point that he asked about her. And when he discovered that she was married, he still sought her company in the solitude of his room.

Following this series of sins, David lost all that he had (2 Samuel 12:10–14). Eventually, the unity David had brought to the house of Israel was destroyed, and the nation suffered much tribulation. A mockery was made of the mighty David, and his name became forever linked to sexual folly.

On the other hand, one of the true heroes of all scripture is Joseph, who was sold by his brothers into captivity in Egypt. His life has many exemplary facets from which we can draw strength and instruction, but one of the most valuable lessons for youth relates to his firm adherence to the law of chastity. He trusted the commandments of the Lord completely when he rejected the repeated sexual advances of his master's wife and fled from her presence. The scorned woman lied, accusing Joseph of accosting her and of fleeing only when she cried out. As a result, Joseph was imprisoned, his life seemingly ruined because of his virtue. But the Lord watched over Joseph, even in prison. By interpreting Pharaoh's dreams, Joseph was elevated to a powerful position in the house of Pharaoh. From this position, he provided for his family several years later during a severe drought (Genesis 39–45).

David tarried, but Joseph got himself out. If you always attend to your duties at school, home, and Church, you will significantly decrease the likelihood of getting into trouble. Joseph understood this principle well, fleeing from a dangerous situation. The Lord rewarded him richly for his wisdom and courage.

Another important lesson to learn from these stories is that thought precedes action. We do not have a record of what these two men thought, but their actions give us some insight. The sight of Bathsheba obviously prompted David to improper thoughts, which he turned into improper actions. Joseph's temptation was even stronger because his master's wife repeatedly sought to entice him. His flight from her advances clearly shows that he did not let the invitation of sin overcome him.

You too must protect your thoughts by avoiding people, places, and things that will lead your mind down dark corridors.

Pick friends and associates who elevate your thoughts and actions. Be found in places and situations for which you will never have to apologize.

In addition, avoid unworthy movies and television shows, tasteless jokes, pornographic websites, sleazy magazines, and so forth. Your mind deserves better input than these sources can offer. They may seem harmless at first, but they are as addictive as any drug, and the results are the same: destroyed self-respect and lost spirituality. If you indulge, you will come away feeling dirty, and no hot shower or bath can make you feel clean. The cost of violating the law of chastity is much too high for short-term pleasure and excitement. Trust in the Lord and in his prophets.

POINTS TO PONDER

- We begin living the law of chastity by carefully controlling our thoughts.
- We control our thoughts by carefully selecting our friends, entertainment, and pastimes.
- The blessings of living the law of chastity are eternal.

CHAPTER 9

Trust in the Law of Tithing

Bring ye all the tithes into the storehouse, that there may be meat in mine house, and prove me now herewith, saith the Lord of hosts, if I will not open you the windows of heaven, and pour you out a blessing, that there shall not be room enough to receive it (Malachi 3:10).

One of the more important decisions you must make is whether to obey the law of tithing. To pay or not to pay, that is the question. This law is simple and easy to understand—pay one-tenth of your annual increase—but not necessarily easy to live unless you gain a testimony of its beauty, blessings, and power. The earlier you gain a testimony of tithing and begin paying it, the easier it will be to obey this law all of your life. Malachi 3:8–12 is the most often quoted scripture on tithing:

"Will a man rob God? Yet ye have robbed me. But ye say, Wherein have we robbed thee? In tithes and offerings. Ye are cursed with a curse: for ye have robbed me, even this whole nation. Bring ye all the tithes into the storehouse, that there may be meat in mine house, and prove me now herewith, saith the Lord of hosts, if I will not open you the windows of heaven, and pour you out a blessing, that there shall not be room enough to receive it. And I will rebuke the devourer for your sakes, and he shall not destroy the fruits of your ground; neither shall your vine cast her fruit before the time in the field, saith the Lord of hosts. And all nations shall call you blessed: for ye shall be a delightsome land, saith the Lord of hosts."

These promises are some of the most direct and bounteous offered anywhere in scripture: More blessings than we can receive! The devourer rebuked for our sakes! Nations calling us blessed! Sounds like a good investment opportunity.

Testimony-strengthening stories about the law of tithing are so abundant that you may wonder why everyone doesn't pay tithing. But a testimony of the law of tithing, as with other gospel principles, usually rests on personal experience rather than on the experience of others. Nonetheless, it is worthwhile to consider a few stories that demonstrate that the Lord keeps his promise to "open . . . the windows of heaven" when we obey this fundamental law.

I have experienced the promises of Malachi in my life. My family has been blessed with a multitude of blessings all of our lives, and we have never wanted for the necessities of life. My patriarchal blessing promises me that if I will remember the Lord with my tithes and offerings, my children, my children's children, and I will never want for the necessities of life. This has been fulfilled in both positive and negative ways. When our children have paid their tithing, they have been blessed with life's necessities; when they have not paid their tithing, they have experienced significant financial difficulties.

One dramatic example occurred after I had left a job with a

large company and had the opportunity to redeem some stock options. At the end of the year, as we were reviewing our finances to ensure that we had paid enough tithing, we discovered that we had paid tithing on a significant amount of money that we were owed but had not yet received. It was an instance of bad book-keeping that I am certain we would not have caught had we not been focused on paying the correct amount of tithing.

While serving as a stake president, I would go home teaching with brethren in the various wards in the stake. One Sunday after-noon we visited an active sister who was married to a supportive but nonmember husband. During the course of our conversation, the sister related that her younger sister had been receiving promptings from their deceased parents to get her life in order and go to the temple to do their temple work. After receiving sev-eral of these promptings, the younger sister committed to go to the temple and complete the temple work for her parents.

After hearing of this commitment, I asked the sister we were visiting, "How about you? When are you going to the temple?" She replied that she couldn't possibly go because she had difficulty paying her tithing. She stated that she was raising her grandson and had to pay a considerable sum of money for day care because she worked full time. I promised her that she could live better on 90 percent than on 100 percent if she gave the difference to the Lord. She thought for a minute and said, "All right, president, you save a space for me on your calendar six months from now, and I will be by for a temple interview."

When we got together six months later for her temple inter-view, this faithful sister related a wonderful story. The same day that she had resumed paying her tithing, a sister in her ward offered to tend her grandson at a rate considerably less than what she had been paying for day care. In fact, the monthly savings was almost exactly the amount that she had paid in tithing. The Lord keeps his promises.

During my service in the presidency of the Africa Southeast Area, a remarkable tithing story came to my attention. At the close of the harvest season, a district president in a farming community sold a tenth of his crop of maize to pay his tithing. That same season, his wife elected not to tithe her harvested maize. They stored their bags of maize side by side in the same location. Before long the wife's untithed maize began to rot, and soon her entire stored crop was ruined. On the other hand, the tithed maize of the district president was preserved in its entirety.

President Gordon B. Hinckley has offered clear and direct guidance on the subject of tithing. He has promised that poor members of the Church will never overcome poverty if they don't pay their tithing. He desires that all Latter-day Saints enjoy the rich blessings that accompany the payment of tithing.

The blessings that flow through the windows of heaven take many shapes and forms, but they do flow. We can trust the Lord to keep his promises.

POINTS TO PONDER

- The Lord will bless you for your obedience to the law of tithing with both temporal and spiritual blessings.
- Early in your life you should "prove [him] now herewith" (Malachi 3:10) so that you can enjoy the blessings that will flow in response to your tithe paying.

CHAPTER 10

Trust in the Word of Wisdom

And all saints who remember to keep and do these sayings, walking in obedience to the commandments, shall receive health in their navel and marrow to their bones; and shall find wisdom and great treasures of knowledge, even hidden treasures; and shall run and not be weary, and shall walk and not faint (D&C 89:18–20).

The Lord has shown his love for us by giving us the Word of Wisdom. Through this law of health, he warns us of substances that can harm our bodies and prevent us from living healthy, productive lives.

When the Lord gave Joseph Smith the Word of Wisdom (D&C 89), the medical world had no understanding of the harmful effects of alcohol, tobacco, coffee, and tea. It was a matter of faith and trust that drove the early Saints to change their habits and live by the concepts of this new law of health. Today we have extensive medical documentation of the damage these substances can do to the body and its functions. To live by the Word of Wisdom is no longer a matter of faith and trust. It is good common sense, substantiated by modern science. To not live by these precepts is a sign of disrespect for our bodies and rebellion against God.

In his book *Stories from My Life,* President James E. Faust shares a powerful account of the blessings that flow from obedience to the Word of Wisdom. When President Faust was president of the Cottonwood Stake in Salt Lake City, Dr. Creed Haymond was the stake patriarch. Dr. Haymond recounted that as a young man he was the captain of his college track team. The night before the most important track meet of the year, his coach instructed the track team to drink a small glass of wine as "a tonic" for their muscles. All of the team members complied with the coach's instructions except Brother Haymond, who had been taught the importance of the Lord's law of health.

"Brother Haymond became very anxious because he did not like to be disobedient to his coach. He was to compete against the fastest men in the world. What if he made a poor showing the next day? How could he face his coach?" wrote President Faust.

"The next day at the track meet the rest of the team members were very ill and performed poorly or were even too sick to run. Brother Haymond, however, felt well and won the 100- and 220-yard dashes. His coach told him, 'You just ran the two hundred and twenty yards in the fastest time it has ever been run by any human being.' That night and for the rest of his life, Creed Haymond was grateful for his simple faith in keeping the Word of Wisdom."[1]

Creed Haymond learned the precepts of the Word of Wisdom at home. The teachings in my home also played a critical role in determining my attitude toward the Lord's law of health. When I was a boy, I used to spend a great deal of time with my grandfather, who lived about a mile away. He was not a member of the Church, and when I was about seven years old he would occasionally give me a taste of beer. I liked it.

I recall going to a café with my grandfather for lunch. We sat down at the counter, and he ordered "a hamburger and a beer." When the waitress asked me what I wanted, I likewise responded, "A hamburger and a beer." She was shocked, and my grandfather was embarrassed. We settled on a hamburger and a root beer for me, much to my disappointment.

When my father heard the story and realized that I had been drinking beer with my grandfather, he was disappointed. He told me that if it happened again I would not be allowed to spend any more time with my grandfather. I loved my grandfather, and I loved to be with him, so the choice was quite easy, even for a seven-year-old. I have not had a drink of beer since then. About that same time, my dad also told me that if he ever caught me smoking he would break my arm. I believed him. Consequently, I never got near a cigarette.

When I arrived at the Air Force Academy, I was surprised at how many of my classmates smoked and how many of the smokers were good athletes. I expected to be able to run faster and farther than any smoker, but it was not so—at least not until after graduation. Several of the smokers and I were later assigned to the same Air Force base, and I watched their smoking catch up with them as we moved into our mid-twenties.

One of those heavy smokers loved to play basketball. As a cadet, he had been able to keep up with most of his classmates for an entire game. But as a twenty-five-year-old, he was good for only three trips up and down the floor. Then he had to take a long rest. Young bodies can put up with a lot of abuse, but eventually bad habits catch up with the abuser with painful, debilitating results. I was so thankful that I had been raised on the Word of Wisdom.

Young people often cite peer pressure and social pressure as reasons for experimenting with substances prohibited by the Word of Wisdom. But pressure doesn't always have to be negative. During my first operational duty assignment, my squadron flew to Buenos Aries, Argentina, in F-100 Super Sabers to participate in the fiftieth anniversary of Argentine air power. One evening in a local restaurant, we had difficulty ordering because none of us spoke Spanish. A gentleman at the next table, seeing our dilemma, came over and assisted us.

After we had been served, a few of the officers at our table sent a bottle of wine to the gentleman's table to show appreciation for his help. He responded by having a two-gallon bottle of wine sent to our table and then joining us with his party. As he proceeded to fill everyone's glass with wine, I told him, "No thanks." He was immediately offended and indicated that I lacked social grace and a sense of hospitality. He was loud, and everyone in the restaurant looked at us.

When he asked me why I would not drink his wine, I told him that it was because of my religion. He then loudly asked, "What kind of religion would stop a man from being sociable?" I answered that I was a Mormon. He immediately grabbed my glass and declared loudly, "Then you had better not drink that wine!"

It turned out that he had been a race car driver for Joey Atwood in Los Angeles in the 1950s and had learned to respect Latter-day Saint values and standards. Once he discovered that I was a Latter-day Saint, he wouldn't have let me drink that wine even if I had wanted to.

I found the same positive pressure when I moved into a fighter squadron on a new base. My boss was a heavy drinker, and I was nervous because I feared that my refusal to drink alcohol would cause problems between us. My fears soon subsided, however, when he called me into his office.

"Bobby, I understand you are a Mormon and don't drink," he said. I nodded in agreement.

"I'll tell you what," he continued. "I won't harass you about your not drinking if you won't harass me about my drinking."

I thought that was a great arrangement, and we started off on what turned out to be a satisfying professional relationship. In fact, I believe that he would have been disappointed in me had he seen me drink.

In today's world tolerance is growing for nondrinkers just as pressure is growing for drinkers not to overindulge. Unfortunately, this positive social pressure is not so prevalent among young people. That is why it is so important for you young men and young women to pick your friends and associates carefully.

When attending the United States Air Force Survival School at Stead Air Force Base in Nevada, I went on a survival trek in the Sierra Nevada Mountains in late September. It was an icy, miserable experience with a lot of cold, wet snow. As we were sitting huddled around a meager fire one cold, wet night, I decided that the powdered coffee in my small packet of survival items might warm me up. I had never tasted coffee, but I was confident that drinking some hot coffee under the circumstances was the smart and correct thing to do.

I heated my canteen cup full of water and poured the coffee powder into it. I then sat back down on my bench—a log that was suspended over two rocks. As I raised the canteen cup toward my mouth, the log broke, dumping me on the ground. The entire cup of coffee went down my front, burning my chest, soaking my jacket, and adding to my misery. Everyone but me had a good laugh. Later, as I reflected on the event, I wondered whether the collapsing log reflected divine intervention. For the rest of the survival trek, I was content to limit my hot drinks to heated water.

The Lord has a multitude of ways to instruct and encourage us along the path of obedience. A good friend of mine in Africa named Bob Eppel was taking the missionary discussions and trying to decide whether to join the Church. One day he determined that he was not going to join, and he told his mother that he was going to quit living the Word of Wisdom. When Bob went to work shortly afterward, his company announced that the drink-dispensing machines had broken down and that there would be no coffee or tea available throughout the day. Bob was less skeptical than I had been at survival school and immediately recognized that the Lord was sending him a message. He joined the Church shortly thereafter.

When my father-in-law joined the Church, he had a difficult time giving up coffee because he liked it so much. One day as he was walking to work, an inspired thought came to his mind: "If the Lord thinks enough of me to give me the Word of Wisdom and tell me that coffee is not good for me, who am I to disagree with him?" He went home, threw out his coffeepot, and fully embraced the Word of Wisdom.

Obedience is what the Lord has always expected of those who hope to stand at his side following the final judgment. Christ, who set an unwavering example of obedience throughout his life, expects us to trust him enough to obey him—even if we must struggle and strive to live his standards.

POINTS TO PONDER

- Modern medicine has validated the wisdom of the Word of Wisdom.
- The Word of Wisdom gives us a heavenly inspired guide to healthful living. It also provides us with an excellent opportunity to demonstrate our ability to master worldly appetites and develop our trust in the Lord.

NOTE

1. James E. Faust, *Stories from My Life* (Salt Lake City: Deseret Book, 2001), 123–24.

CHAPTER 11

Trust in the Lord through Service

And behold, I tell you these things that ye may learn wisdom; that ye may learn that when ye are in the service of your fellow beings ye are only in the service of your God (Mosiah 2:17).

L ife is full, and many conflicting activities vie for your time and attention. In your youth, you make choices that often determine your priorities for the rest of your life. Consequently, in making your choices and setting your goals, don't forget to make some time to serve the Lord. The most obvious way for young men, and some young women, to serve the Lord is through full-time missionary service. Dedicated mission service is life changing, which is why we have come to expect returned missionaries to describe their missions as "the best two years of my life."

The beauty and satisfaction of service to the Lord goes far beyond serving a mission while you're young. You can enjoy the rich blessings of service throughout your life as you accept and faithfully fulfill the many Church callings that will inevitably come to you as an active Latter-day Saint. The common admonition to "magnify your calling" is a key to securing satisfaction by committing yourself to superior Church service.

On occasion the Lord will bless you in surprising ways because of your willingness to serve in his Church. While I was taking fighter gunnery training at Luke Air Force Base near Phoenix, Arizona, in 1960, I was called to serve as the deacons quorum adviser, a calling I thoroughly enjoyed. One weekend we went on an overnight camping trip south of Phoenix near the Eagle Tail Mountains, an interesting and unique range that I enjoyed seeing up close.

A few weeks later, I was flying a low-level navigation check ride in a two-seated training model of the F-100. I had flown the high-altitude portion of the flight on instruments, using a hood to prevent me from looking outside and keeping oriented with the ground. After we had completed our letdown, the instructor told me to come out from under the hood and fly the low-level portion of the flight to the target using ground references.

I was greatly dismayed to find that I was nowhere near where I had expected to be. I had clearly let down in the wrong place. But my dismay quickly turned to relief when I recognized my new friends, the Eagle Tail Mountains. I was quickly able to orient myself, get back on course, and find the target—right on time. The instructor was amazed at my navigation skill, but I was amazed at my good fortune. It worked out because I had spent a night at the foot of the Eagle Tails with my deacons quorum. For my willingness to serve as called, I had received a special blessing.

A couple of years later, I was blessed for my Church service in a much more subtle but nonetheless impressive way. In Las Vegas I had been called to be the second counselor in the bishopric of a newly formed ward, and we were busy putting the ward's organization together. At the same time, I received a new job as the operations officer in a fighter squadron at nearby Nellis Air Force Base. As I spent time at work trying to reorganize the operations function in the squadron, I quickly learned an important lesson. I realized that the same techniques used to interview people before extending Church callings also worked in making squadron assignments.

I spent all week at work and all weekend at Church interviewing people. The only hitch occurred one Monday morning following a Sunday of Church interviews. I inadvertently asked a captain at work if he would kneel with me and offer a prayer. He looked at me with surprise and seemed relieved when I mumbled something about "dispensing with prayer this morning."

In retrospect, we probably would have been better off had we prayed at work as well as at Church. But that little hiccup aside, at the end of the restructuring I appreciated the organizational instruction and experience I had received in Church. Again the Lord had blessed me in an unexpected way for my willingness to serve.

Opportunities and obligations to serve others abound and vary widely throughout our lives. They sometimes come with high visibility and wide acclaim, but most often they are quiet acts, performed on unheralded stages to small audiences.

My uncle Wilbur Oaks passed away a few years ago after spending ten years in a coma in a care center. Each day of those ten years his wife, Aunt Ethel, went to the center and helped nurse him. After Uncle Wilbur's passing, I had an opportunity to express my admiration to Aunt Ethel for her diligent, exemplary service. Her response was sweet and revealing: "It was no big thing. He would have done the same for me." Kind, compassionate service has a powerful way of bringing out the best in us and of prompting us to see the best in others whom we serve.

Some of the greatest service opportunities that come to Latter-day Saints come in conjunction with home and visiting teaching assignments. Through faithful home teachers, less-active members are flushed out, fellowshipped, and brought again into full activity; "till-death-do-us-part" couples are persuaded to prepare their families to be sealed in the temple; and young men and young women are linked with new sets of gospel-involved friends. All of this and more can be accomplished through diligent and reliable home and visiting teaching.

When one of our daughters-in-law was called as a visiting teacher in Little Rock, Arkansas, she was assigned to visit a sister whose antagonistic husband would stomp through the house, go outside to the carport, and smoke until she left. One day after eighteen months of visiting this sister, who also smoked, our daughter-in-law talked with her about the challenges of life, commenting that if everyone's sins smelled like cigarette smoke, most people would stink. The sister, who had stopped going to Church because she had resumed smoking and didn't feel worthy around other Latter-day Saints, had never thought about her problem in that way. Soon after this discussion, the sister returned to Church.

Our daughter-in-law asked that this sister be assigned as her visiting teaching companion despite the sister's feelings of inadequacy and unworthiness. She reluctantly accepted the calling and was soon offering prayers and giving lessons. A couple of years later, our son and daughter-in-law traveled to the Dallas Texas

Temple with this sister. Her antagonistic husband has warmed to the Church and now allows the members to enter their home and share gospel messages. The beginning of this warming occurred when the elders quorum visited the home to cut down a few trees. The husband could not believe that someone would go to so much trouble to help him in such a meaningful way.

Diligent, productive service can be a long process. If our daughter-in-law had become discouraged and given up on this sister after sixteen or seventeen months, no one would ever have known why she had quit coming to Church. This sister needed and responded to a true service-oriented friend, not just a monthly visit. Although our son and his family have moved from Little Rock, they stay in touch with this sister and remain good friends with her.

King Benjamin, the powerful and wise Book of Mormon leader, put service in near perfect perspective in the opening words of his beautiful discourse to his people: "And behold, I tell you these things that ye may learn wisdom; that ye may learn that when ye are in the service of your fellow beings ye are only in the service of your God" (Mosiah 2:17). Is it not reasonable to expect that our loving Father in Heaven would give special blessings to those who faithfully serve him by giving dedicated service to his sons and daughters?

The Lord set the standard of service and defined the bounds of the term *neighbor* in his parable of the good Samaritan. A traveler who was robbed, beaten, and left to die on the road to Jericho was passed by and ignored by a priest and a Levite, men who should have had charity in their hearts. Instead, the traveler was nursed and cared for by a Samaritan, who had every right to be hostile or, at best, uninterested. We do not know what reward the Samaritan received for his service, but the implication is that he found a reward in heaven (Luke 10:30–37).

In the final hours of his ministry on earth, Jesus gave a clear and vivid declaration on the saving power that we draw upon when we provide service to our neighbors:

"Then shall the King say unto them on his right hand, Come, ye blessed of my Father, inherit the kingdom prepared for you from the foundation of the world: for I was an hungred, and ye gave me meat: I was thirsty, and ye gave me drink: I was a stranger, and ye took me in: naked, and ye clothed me: I was sick, and ye visited me: I was in prison, and ye came unto me.

"Then shall the righteous answer him, saying, Lord, when saw we thee an hungred, and fed thee? Or thirsty, and gave thee drink? When saw we thee a stranger, and took thee in? Or naked, and clothed thee? Or when saw we thee sick, or in prison, and came unto thee? And the King shall answer and say unto them, Verily I say unto you, inasmuch as ye have done it unto one of the least of these my brethren, ye have done it unto me" (Matthew 25:34–40).

If you would be numbered among the King's sheep and blessed to "inherit the kingdom prepared for you from the foundation of the world," you must become sensitive to the needs of your neighbor. And you must be willing to serve when you perceive a need. Such is the Lord's way.

You do not need to travel up and down the road to Jericho looking for needy neighbors. Fellow travelers who need your help live next door and in your ward. Understand that the service you render by magnifying your Church callings is deemed just as important as helping a battered victim you may find along the road. To feed the hungry soul who shows up in your Primary or in your Young Women or Young Men class is one of the most effective, important acts of service that you can render.

We should cherish the callings that give us the opportunity to nurture others by the good word of God. These experiences, coupled with acts of charitable service, help us develop a Christlike character.

POINTS TO PONDER

- When you trust the Lord's many admonitions to serve others, you build for yourself treasure in heaven.
- You can find great personal satisfaction from each act of Christian service that you render.

CHAPTER 12

Trust in the Lord through Missionary Work

Go ye therefore, and teach all nations, baptizing them in the name of the Father, and of the Son, and of the Holy Ghost (Matthew 28:19).

Missionary work has been a part of the gospel throughout recorded history. As the Old Testament prophets went about calling people to repentance, they became the early model of the dedicated missionary. Christ himself spent much of his life teaching all who would listen to his words of eternal truth and happiness, and he sent his apostles to teach the gospel to all nations, "baptizing them in the name of the Father, and of the Son, and of the Holy Ghost" (Matthew 28:19).

When the gospel of Jesus Christ was restored and the Church organized in these latter days, one of the first things the Prophet Joseph Smith did was to send forth missionaries to share truths and testimonies with the honest in heart. That work has moved forward since 1830 and will continue as long as dedicated Latter-day Saints, both young and old, are willing to sacrifice their time, energy, and resources.

President Gordon B. Hinckley has advised us to never underestimate the power and reach of our missionary work. His words should prompt us to seek for opportunities to share with our family and friends the life-changing truths of the restored gospel of Jesus Christ. Some of the most satisfying moments in life come through having someone we know or love accept the gospel and enter into the waters of baptism.

Repeatedly in scripture, the Lord calls his people to go forth and teach his gospel. One of the most direct and exciting of these callings is found in the Doctrine and Covenants. Trusting in the Lord and in his promised blessings, thousands and thousands of young men and young women have gone forth as missionaries armed with these verses:

"Wherefore, you are called to cry repentance unto this people. And if it so be that you should labor all your days in crying repentance unto this people, and bring, save it be one soul unto me, how great shall be your joy with him in the kingdom of my Father! And now, if your joy will be great with one soul that you have brought unto me into the kingdom of my Father, how great will be your joy if you should bring many souls unto me!" (D&C 18:14–16).

The Doctrine and Covenants offers further emphasis and instruction on proclaiming the gospel in subsequent sections:

"And ye shall go forth in the power of my Spirit, preaching my gospel, two by two, in my name, lifting up your voices as with the sound of a trump, declaring my word like unto angels of God. And ye shall go forth baptizing with water, saying: Repent ye, repent ye, for the kingdom of heaven is at hand" (D&C 42:6–7).

"Behold, I sent you out to testify and warn the people, and it becometh every man who hath been warned to warn his neighbor. Therefore, they are left without excuse, and their sins are upon their own heads" (D&C 88:81–82).

From my personal missionary experience, I know that rich blessings flow to us when we overcome our fears and open our mouths to share truths that bounteously bless our lives. In the summer of 2000, as my wife and I were preparing to depart for an assignment to serve in the South Africa Area Presidency in Johannesburg, South Africa, we traveled to San Francisco to visit our daughter Kristie for a few days. During our visit, I was asked to speak at a fireside in a young single adult ward. As I was sitting on the stand waiting for the meeting to begin, I asked the young counselor in the bishopric who was conducting the meeting what his name was and where he was from. He replied that he was Brother Ogilvie, from Minneapolis, Minnesota. I paused and asked him if he was related to Dr. James Ogilvie, who taught at the University of Minnesota. "He is my father," he replied.

For a few moments, I was unable to speak. As an upperclassman at the Air Force Academy during the 1958–59 school year, I counseled younger students regarding their academic plans. One young cadet named James Ogilvie was contemplating leaving the academy in order to enter a premedical undergraduate program and then go to medical school. During the course of our counseling sessions, we discussed the restored gospel. As a result, James Ogilvie received the missionary discussions, accepted the gospel, and was baptized. He raised his family in the Church, and each of his sons served a full-time mission. As I realized the impact that the conversion of James had on many lives, I felt richly blessed for my missionary efforts several years before.

President Richard Siems, of the Cape Town Stake in Cape Town, South Africa, told me a story of the 1928 conversion of his grandmother. His story underscores President Hinckley's admonition to never underestimate the power and reach of your missionary work. President Siems's grandmother was married and raising her four young children in Cape Town when one day she became extremely ill. Doctors, who declared that they could do nothing to save her life, diagnosed her illness as food poisoning.

While she was lying in bed surrounded by concerned family members, a knock came at the door. Two young men had arrived with a message about the Lord Jesus Christ. The father of the house told the Latter-day Saint missionaries that his family was in crisis and had no time for religious discussions. He then asked them to leave. After the missionaries had ridden away on their bicycles, the father returned to his wife's bedside.

"Who was that?" his wife asked before he had a chance to sit down.

"A couple of young men who wanted to talk about religion. Why?"

"Call them back," she answered. "When you opened the door, I felt something."

The husband moved quickly to the door, but it was too late; the missionaries had disappeared. But the same Spirit that radiated from the missionaries at the door prompted them to stop their bikes in the middle of the street and return to the home. When they knocked on the door this time, they were warmly welcomed and introduced to the dying mother. After hearing the diagnosis, they called their mission president, who immediately came to help them give the woman a priesthood blessing. The medically hopeless mother quickly recovered and was back at work the next day.

Not surprising, the family soon joined the Church and subsequently raised their large family in the gospel. Four generations of Latter-day Saints from this family have generated missionaries, stake presidents, bishops, branch presidents, elders quorum presidents, Relief Society presidents, and numerous other Church leaders. This contribution to the kingdom can be attributed to two worthy young men responding to the Lord's call to go forth and preach the gospel to the world. Never underestimate the power of your missionary efforts, no matter how feeble and futile they may seem.

The Church's army of missionaries spreading the sweet message of the restored gospel across the face of the earth is a miracle. This army is primarily made up of young men and young women who are willing to lose their lives for a time so that others may enjoy the peace and joy that they have found in the restored gospel. Through their testimony and conviction, they move forward the work to prepare the earth for the return of the Savior. Trust in the Lord and join the ranks of this miracle army.

POINTS TO PONDER

- The Lord entrusts most of his missionary work, one of the most important responsibilities of the restored gospel, to young men and young women.
- For Latter-day Saints, few activities in life are as satisfying as sharing the restored truths of the gospel of Jesus Christ.

CHAPTER 13

Trust in the Lord's Atonement

For we labor diligently to write, to persuade our children, and also our brethren, to believe in Christ, and to be reconciled to God; for we know that it is by grace that we are saved, after all we can do (2 Nephi 25:23).

Our trust and faith would mean little in the grand scheme of life if not for the Atonement. This marvelous gift from our Father in Heaven comes to us through the atoning sacrifice of his Only Begotten Son in the Garden of Gethsemane and on the cross at Calvary. To trust with conviction and to have unfaltering faith, we must understand how central the Atonement is to the plan of salvation. We must also understand the essential role the Atonement plays in giving us the opportunity to return to the presence of our Father in Heaven.

THE PLAN OF HAPPINESS

In the premortal councils in heaven, our Father presented to us his plan of happiness, known as the plan of salvation. This plan was designed to provide us with the opportunity to return to his presence and dwell with him eternally in a celestial sphere. We all accepted and supported the proposed plan, which called for each of us to come to earth so that we could achieve two major objectives. First, we needed to obtain a physical body of flesh and bones. Second, we had to be tested outside the presence and direct influence of our Father in Heaven.

We needed the opportunity to exercise our moral agency, either yielding to the vast array of temptations Satan would lay before us or following "the enticings of the Holy Spirit, and [putting] off the natural man and [becoming] a saint through the atonement of Christ the Lord" (Mosiah 3:19).

By obtaining a body and being tested, we prepare ourselves to return to the presence of our Father in Heaven as celestial beings. Moses 1:39 helps us understand the importance of this plan: "For behold, this is my work and my glory—to bring to pass the immortality and eternal life of man."

THE FALL

To move the plan of salvation forward, we had to accept it and then leave our heavenly home. Our exit was accomplished through the fall of Adam and Eve in the Garden of Eden.

"Adam's fall brought spiritual and temporal death into the world," Elder Bruce R. McConkie wrote. "*Spiritual death* is to be cast out of the presence of the Lord (2 Nephi 9:6) and to die as pertaining to things of righteousness, or in other words things of the Spirit (Helaman 14:15–18). *Temporal death* or natural death is the separation of body and spirit, the body going back to the dust from which it was created and the spirit to a world of waiting spirits to await the day of the resurrection."[1]

THE LAW OF JUSTICE

In our spiritually dead testing state, known as mortality or earth life, we inevitably make wrong choices and break divine laws. By violating God's laws, we become imperfect or blemished. Obviously we must become clean before we can return to God because no unclean thing can dwell in his presence (1 Nephi 10:21; Moses 6:57).

"According to the terms and conditions of the great plan of redemption, *justice demands that a penalty be paid for every viola-tion of the Lord's laws,*" Elder McConkie added. "This necessarily must be so or this mortal existence could not fulfil its purpose as a probationary and preparatory state. Since mortal man is on pro-bation to prepare himself for eternity, and since he is endowed with the great gift of free agency, it follows that he must be held accountable for his disobedience. Otherwise this sphere of exis-tence would not provide the test nor give the experience which would qualify him to return to the presence of God hereafter."[2]

Where a law is given, a penalty is assigned for every violation of that law, in accordance with the law of justice. In speaking to his errant son, Corianton, Alma clearly outlined this truth: "If not so, the works of justice would be destroyed, and God would cease to be God. . . . Behold, justice exerciseth all his demands" (Alma 42:22, 24).

THE LAW OF MERCY

The good news is that the mercy of God allows the punitive demands of justice to be met "by an infinite sacrifice by the shedding of blood," taught President Joseph Fielding Smith. "For this purpose Jesus Christ came into the world, for he had volunteered in the pre-existence to come and die that we might live."[3]

The atonement of Jesus Christ is at the heart of the cleansing process. It satisfies the law of justice. The pain and agony of Gethsemane and Calvary suffered by the unblemished Lamb of God provides, in a miraculous but unfathomable way, sufficient payment for all of the sins and suffering of all humanity—past, present, and future. The only stipulation placed on the receipt of this magnificent gift is that the recipient honor the gift and the giver through the process known as repentance.

Repentance requires the sorrowful acknowledgment of sin, including confession when necessary; the complete turning from sin, to return no more; the restitution of the damage caused by sin, where possible; and the diligent striving to keep all of the Lord's commandments. Through the law of mercy, the demands of the law of justice upon the sinner are paid vicariously by the suffering of Jesus Christ.

The second great and glorious gift flowing from the Atonement is that temporal death, the separation of the mortal body and the spirit, is conquered for all. Through the resurrection of Christ, "the temporal death of the fall is replaced by the state of immortality which comes because of the atonement and resurrection of our Lord. The body and spirit which separated, incident to . . . the natural death, are reunited in immortality, in an inseparable connection."[4]

Jacob, the brother of Nephi, summed up the impact of the law of mercy on physical death when he wrote: "For as death hath passed upon all men, to fulfil the merciful plan of the great Creator, there must needs be a power of resurrection, and the resurrection must needs come unto man by reason of the fall; and the fall came by reason of transgression; and because man became fallen they were cut off from the presence of the Lord.

"Wherefore, it must needs be an infinite atonement—save it should be an infinite atonement this corruption could not put on incorruption. Wherefore, the first judgment which came upon man must needs have remained to an endless duration. And if so, this flesh must have laid down to rot and to crumble to its mother earth, to rise no more. O the wisdom of God, his mercy and grace!" (2 Nephi 9:6–8).

The success of the Father's plan of happiness rested upon the willingness of Christ to voluntarily submit himself to the demands of justice, atoning for the fall of Adam and Eve and for all those who would repent of their sins. As Elder McConkie has written, "If there had been no atonement of Christ (there having been a fall of Adam!), then the whole plan and purpose connected with the creation of man would have come to naught. If there had been no atonement, temporal death would have remained forever, and there never would have been a resurrection. The body would have remained forever in the grave, and the spirit would have stayed in a spirit prison to all eternity. If there had been no atonement, there never would have been spiritual or eternal life for any persons. Neither mortals nor spirits could have been cleansed from sin, and all the spirit hosts of heaven would have wound up as devils, angels to a devil."[5]

President Marion G. Romney beautifully summed up the wonderful interaction of the law of justice, the law of mercy, and the Atonement. "All have sinned," he said. "Each person is therefore unclean to the extent to which he has sinned, and because of that uncleanness is banished from the presence of the Lord so long as the effect of his own wrongdoing is upon him.

"Since we suffer this spiritual death as a result of our own transgressions, we cannot claim deliverance therefrom as a matter of justice. Neither has any man the power within himself alone to make restitution so complete that he can be wholly cleansed from the effect of his own wrongdoing. If men are to be freed from the results of their own transgressions and brought back into the presence of God, they must be the beneficiaries of some expedient beyond themselves which will free them from the effects of their own sins. For this purpose was the atonement of Jesus Christ conceived and executed."[6]

A soul so great and so giving as Jesus Christ, our Lord and our Savior, is truly deserving of our trust, faith, and eternal gratitude. Each of our days should contain moments dedicated to offering up our most heartfelt thanks for this great gift, his atoning sacrifice.

POINTS TO PONDER

- "It is by grace that we are saved, after all we can do" (2 Nephi 25:23).
- The atonement of Jesus Christ is central to Christian theology.
- The Only Begotten Son of God is eternally deserving of our gratitude.

NOTES

1. Bruce R. McConkie, *Mormon Doctrine* (Salt Lake City: Deseret Book, 1966), 62.

2. Ibid., 406.

3. Joseph Fielding Smith, *Doctrines of Salvation,* comp. Bruce R. McConkie, 3 vols. (Salt Lake City: Bookcraft, 1954–56), 1:122.

4. McConkie, 62.

5. Ibid., 63.

6. Marion G. Romney, "The Resurrection of Jesus," *Ensign,* April 1982, 8.

CHAPTER 14

Trust in the Lord in Your Decisions

Trust in the Lord with all thine heart; and lean not unto thine own understanding. In all thy ways acknowledge him, and he shall direct thy paths (Proverbs 3:5–6).

You face some tough decisions as a young Latter-day Saint, but you have help in making the right decisions. The Lord can ease your uncertainty and give you confidence, purpose, and direction if you learn of him and accept his plan. Decisions become easier when you arm yourself with gospel answers to such questions as "Where did I come from?" "Why am I here?" and "Where am I going?"

Gospel knowledge gives you a standard by which to judge the alternatives you will face in life. For example, if you believe in and are striving for eternal life in God's presence, you will pursue those paths that lead you toward that goal. I have a strong testimony that the restored gospel of Jesus Christ will lead us to that grand and glorious reward.

Let's consider some of the specific questions that face most young men and young women: "Whom should I choose as friends?" "How often should I attend Church?" "How much attention should I pay to the Word of Wisdom, the law of chastity, the law of tithing, and observance of the Sabbath day?" "Should I go to college?" "Should I go on a mission?" "When, where, and whom should I marry?"

An important part of wise decision making is gathering as much information as possible before deciding which path to take. Attractive, unmarked paths in a forest can lead to a dead end, to the foot of a steep mountain you're not prepared to climb, or to a treacherous snake-infested swamp. You can find out where the paths you are considering will lead you by appealing to the Lord. He is an experienced trail guide who knows the best routes through life's unfamiliar paths.

When I was a cadet, I had a big decision to make about marriage. My girlfriend, Gloria Unger, and I had been dating for many years but had made no commitment regarding marriage. I realized that it was time to either make a commitment or move on. It so happened at the time that I had an assignment in English class to write a decision-making paper on an actual problem.

As silly as it now sounds, I decided to write a paper on whether to marry Gloria. I listed all of the pros and cons, discussing them in detail and weighing the alternatives. I turned the paper in and got a C+. Fortunately, I threw it away before I got married. I don't even remember the conclusion to which my absurdly scientific analysis led me, but a few months later I asked Gloria to marry me. That was forty-four years ago. I now know that I would have stood on much surer ground had I fasted, knelt in prayer, and sought the Lord's guidance and counsel in this important matter.

Another important part of decision making is timeliness. When we hesitate in making decisions, we find that our choices quickly narrow. We hesitate asking a young lady to dance, only to find that a few moments later she is in someone else's arms. We debate whether to buy an attractive dress in a store window, only to return later and find that it has already been sold.

There will always be another dance and another dress, but for some of the most important decisions that you must make, there may not be a second chance to make the right decision. With respect to college, the Word of Wisdom, friends, the law of chastity, a mission, and marriage, you may only get one chance to take the high path.

SHOULD I GO TO COLLEGE?

The scriptural statement that "the glory of God is intelligence" (D&C 93:36) helps you understand the importance of seeking knowledge throughout your life. Further, modern-day prophets have urged young people to prepare to provide for themselves and their families, admonishing them to pursue adequate schooling as a part of their preparation.

"The difference between no high school degree and a high school graduate is an average income increase of 38 percent," said Elder L. Tom Perry. "From a high school diploma to some college, the increase is 20 percent, and from a high school diploma to a university degree, the increase is 56 percent. Yes, education does pay. It is never too early to determine the direction you want to prepare yourself for."[1]

HOW STRICTLY SHOULD I HEED THE DO'S AND DON'TS OF THE WORD OF WISDOM?

Modern prophets speak with one voice regarding the importance of avoiding the destructive force of addictive substances such as alcohol, tobacco, and hard drugs. They always sustain the admonitions and powerful promises found in the Word of Wisdom. But their admonitions are no longer voices in the wilderness on these matters. Modern medicine and death notices have emphatically documented the practical value of living by the teachings of the Word of Wisdom. It makes good health sense, good economic sense, and good obedience sense. It also makes good spiritual sense.

Elder Joseph B. Wirthlin has observed, "When we obey the Word of Wisdom, windows of personal revelation are opened to us and our souls are filled with divine light and truth."[2]

HOW CHOOSY SHOULD I BE WHEN IT COMES TO FRIENDS?

You are likely familiar with the sayings "Birds of a feather flock together" and "A man is known by the company he keeps." But you may be less familiar with a scripture that highlights the impact our friends may have on us. "Make no friendship with an angry man; and with a furious man thou shalt not go: Lest thou learn his ways, and get a snare to thy soul" (Proverbs 22:24–25).

You will receive strength from the Lord and grow in his ways if you choose to associate with people who love him and desire to heed his counsel and direction. They will give you needed support as you seek to pattern your life after gospel ideals. President Thomas S. Monson has counseled, "Friends help to determine your future. You will tend to be like them and to be found where they choose to go. . . . The friends you choose will either help or hinder your success."[3]

IS THE LAW OF CHASTITY REALLY THAT IMPORTANT?

The scriptures and modern-day prophets give clear and unmistakable guidance on the importance of living a morally pure life. Your happiness in this life and in the life to come depends on your willingness to embrace this law, be true to your covenants, and prove faithful to your future spouse.

Counsel from latter-day prophets includes strong warnings on avoiding pornography. President Gordon B. Hinckley said, "Pornography is the literature of the devil. Shun it. Stay away from it. Lift your sights and your minds to the higher and nobler things of life. Remember, 'wickedness never was happiness' (Alma 41:10). Sin never brought happiness. Transgression never brought happiness. Disobedience never brought happiness."[4]

SHOULD I SERVE A MISSION?

Heavenly counsel to Orson Pratt through the prophet Joseph Smith reflects the Lord's will and promise for missionary service. "And more blessed are you because you are called of me to preach my gospel—To lift up your voice as with the sound of a trump, both long and loud, and cry repentance unto a crooked and perverse generation, preparing the way of the Lord for his second coming" (D&C 34:5–6).

If you will trust in the Lord's counsel, you will find great growth and deep satisfaction throughout your life. Modern prophets have declared that every worthy young man should prepare himself to serve a full-time mission. Young women may also serve missions, but "missionary work is essentially a priesthood responsibility," said President Hinckley. "As such, our young men must carry the major burden. This is their responsibility and their obligation."[5]

WHY DO WE TALK SO MUCH ABOUT MARRIAGE IN THE CHURCH?

The questions surrounding marriage—when, where, and to whom—are so key to your happiness in this life and through the eternities that they should be addressed often and always in a context of diligently praying and seeking guidance from the Lord. He will help you make decisions of timing, location, and partner on the basis of his eternal criteria and love for you.

All young people looking for answers can find relevant counsel and guidance in the scriptures, from the modern prophets, and through the Holy Ghost. Seek God's guidance and then listen closely for his instructions. When you follow a pattern of seeking the Lord's confirmation and will, you will avoid many of the pitfalls that beset so many young people today.

POINTS TO PONDER

- Young men and women around the world face many of life's most important decisions while in their youth.
- The scriptures, the prophets, and the Holy Ghost provide powerful guidance by which to make decisions.

NOTES

1. L. Tom Perry, "Youth of the Noble Birthright," *Ensign,* November 1998, 74.
2. Joseph B. Wirthlin, "Windows of Light and Truth," *Ensign,* November 1995, 76.

3. Thomas S. Monson, "In Harm's Way," *Ensign,* May 1998, 47.
4. Gordon B. Hinckley, in "What Prophets and Apostles Teach about Chastity and Fidelity," *Ensign,* October 1998, 38.
5. Gordon B. Hinckley, "Some Thoughts on Temples, Retention of Converts, and Missionary Service," *Ensign,* November 1997, 52.

CHAPTER 15

For Strength, Trust in the Arm of the Lord

The Lord is my rock, and my fortress, and my deliverer; the God of my rock; in him will I trust (2 Samuel 22:2–3).

This book began with a discussion about the importance of placing our trust in the arm of the Lord rather than in the arm of flesh. Preceding chapters have discussed the importance of trusting in prayer, the word of the Lord, obedience, chastity, tithing, the Word of Wisdom, service, missionary work, the Atonement, and righteous decisions. As you've learned by now, strength flows from this trust.

For example, physical strength can come through the ordinance of priesthood administration to the sick. That might not be the kind of strength you are seeking, but if you have ever participated in or witnessed the healing power of the priesthood on behalf of a sick person, you know that real power and strength were made manifest. This power is only available through a righteous, faithful priesthood holder.

Prayer is another great source of strength. When we consider the Lord's promises to answer our prayers and give us what we seek from him in righteousness, we have the strength of the Lord standing squarely behind us!

Trust in the word of God. When you do this, you have access to all of the wisdom, counsel, and direction of four books of scripture, a host of modern prophets, and the Holy Ghost to help you with your decisions and challenges. The word of the Lord can give you strength and wisdom to solve even the most difficult problems. If you habitually turn to these sources for help, you will walk through life with a confident stride, knowing that you are drawing upon the all-knowing wisdom of God the Eternal Father to help you. That is powerful!

The strength available through obedience is, in many cases, the easiest to understand. The promises contained in the Word of Wisdom are straightforward promises of strength. "And all saints who remember to keep and do these sayings, walking in obedience to the commandments, shall receive health in their navel and marrow to their bones." Any doctor will attest to the fact that bone marrow is essential to a strong and healthy body. Easier to appreciate are the promises to "run and not be weary" and to "walk and not faint." The Word of Wisdom promises what many people spend time and money on: physical fitness. The marvelous promise of walking without becoming faint, meanwhile, may have special significance to the elderly (D&C 89:18, 20).

But the Word of Wisdom is not just about physical strength. "And shall find wisdom and great treasures of knowledge, even hidden treasures" (D&C 89:19) is a promise that reaches far beyond the physical. Hidden treasures of wisdom and knowledge are assets that prove valuable in any endeavor in life.

Strength derived through service is more subtle and difficult to quantify. But a careful review of the lives of great leaders discloses their focus on the well-being of their people and a dedication to their success. People are eager to follow leaders who sacrifice for others and who forget their self-interest. The Lord has many ways to reward you when you forget yourself and serve others with enthusiasm.

We could go through virtually every commandment and demonstrate that obedience brings us strength and power as we move through life. This makes perfect sense. We show our faith and trust in the Lord primarily through our willingness to follow his direction and commandments. His blessings of strength and power come to us as a direct result of our living in accordance with eternal principles.

Trust is a wonderful word. We begin our lives in a cocoon of trust. We trust that there will be food, shelter, protection, and love within the confines of our family. We start school trusting that teachers will teach true and valuable lessons. We select friends whom we feel we can trust. We trust brands of food, clothing, and other items that we purchase. We date young men and young women whom we trust and with whom we trust ourselves.

Why is trust so important? Within the sheltering circle of trust, we can relax, rest easy, and be at peace. We have no cause to feel tense or threatened.

Unfortunately we all experience disappointment when our trust is broken or misplaced. The cocoon of family protection can break down, and our food, shelter, protection, and love can be lost. At school we find that some teachers put agendas before truth. Trusted name brands aren't always trustworthy. Not everyone we date is worthy of our trust.

The roots of cynicism are easy to trace to broken trust, and fuel to feed the fire of distrust and suspicion is ample. But distrust and suspicion are miserable paths to walk. We cannot relax, rest easy, or be at peace on such paths. We must constantly look over our shoulder, worrying about who is going to let us down next. That is not a happy trip.

But from a gospel perspective, our glass is not half empty. Rather, it is more than half full, no matter what our personal history and circumstances. When we accept the Atonement as God's great gift to us, our cup indeed runneth over. We all have the opportunity to repent of our sins, we all will be raised from the grave, and we all will have the privilege of dwelling in the presence of the Father and the Son, sharing all that they have.

The Lord is the one sure, trustworthy being in our lives. Alma the Younger voiced his firm conviction of the dependability of God: "I do know that whosoever shall put their trust in God shall be supported in their trials, and their troubles, and their afflictions, and shall be lifted up at the last day" (Alma 36:3).

Alma's son Helaman heard his father's words and learned of him. In his adult life he was called upon to lead the 2,060 stripling warriors in numerous battles. As he described the source of the strength of those marvelous warriors, he highlighted the importance of trust. "Now this was the faith of these of whom I have spoken; they are young, and their minds are firm, and they do put their trust in God continually" (Alma 57:27). Trusting in their mothers and in their God, they fought battles in which thousands of their enemies were killed while not a single one of them lost his life.

"But behold, we trust in our God who has given us victory over those lands," Helaman said later, "insomuch that we have obtained those cities and those lands, which were our own" (Alma 58:33).

God will never let down a trusting servant. In his protecting circle, you will find strength, power, and peace. That is why you must not let the trust-destroying experiences of the world rob you of your ability to trust in him whose love "never faileth" (Moroni 7:46).

On the basis of experiences in my life and in the lives of others I have observed, I encourage you to put the Lord and his promises to the test. Believe him! Trust him! Have faith in him! Follow his ways and directions! By so doing, you will find strength, power, peace, and answers.

These blessings may be as immediate as when I uttered a desperate prayer during a dinner in Leningrad, they may be delayed a couple of weeks as when I excitedly sighted the Eagle Tail Mountains in Arizona, or they may take much longer, even a lifetime. But the Lord's blessings will come to you and bear witness that he is there, today and always, to guide and help each of his children with their challenges—including you with yours.

Your Father in Heaven loves you beyond your ability to imagine, and he wants only the best for you. He deserves your deepest trust all the days of your life. And for your trust, he will richly reward you.

Index

Actions, thoughts preceding, 70–71

Adam and Eve, 13, 32

Arm of flesh, 17–21

Arm of Lord, 115–19

Atonement, 99–104

Atwood, Joey, 80

Bathsheba, 68–69

Beer, 78–79

Benson, Ezra Taft, on Book of Mormon, 39

Berlin, prayer in, 32–33

Bible, 35–36

Book of Mormon, 10, 31, 37, 38, 39–40, 60, 63

Callings, 85–87

Cannon, George Q., on Lord's trust in youth, 12

Chastity, 67–71, 111

Coffee, 81–82

College, 109

David, fall of, 68–70

David and Goliath, 10, 19–20

Death, atonement and, 102–3

Decision making, 107–12

Disappointment, 1–7

Education, 109

Elisha, 56

Eppel, Bob, 82

Faith, obedience and, 49–56,
  59–60. *See also* Trust
Fall of Adam, 13, 100
Faust, James E., on Creed
  Haymond, 78
Flesh, arm of, 17–21
Flying, 3–5; faith and, 50–52
Food poisoning, blessing for,
  96–97
Football, 1–3
Friends, choosing, 110–11

Good Samaritan, the, 89–90
Gospel, sharing, 93–97

Happiness: foundation of,
  13–14; plan of, 99–100
Haymond, Creed, Word of
  Wisdom and, 78
Healing, of sick mother,
  96–97
Hinckley, Gordon B.:
  confidence of, in youth,
  11; on "chosen
  generation," 12; as
  prophet, 41, 42; on
  missionary work, 94, 96,
  112; on pornography, 111
Holy Ghost, 43–47
Home teaching, 88–89
Honors, worldly and
  heavenly, 5–7

Jesus Christ, 10, 15, 32, 63,
  90, 96, 101–2, 104
Joseph, son of Jacob, 70
Justice, law of, 101

Kimball, Spencer W., 42
King Benjamin, 89
King David, 68–69

Lee, Harold B., 39
Leningrad, 27–28
Log, breaking, 81–82
Lord: love of, for youth,
  9–11; arm of, 115–19

Maize, story of, 76
Marriage, 108, 112
Mary, 11–12
Maynes, Alden, 28–31
McConkie, Bruce R.: on Fall,
  100; on justice, 101; on
  Atonement, 103
Mercy, law of, 101–4
Missionary work, 93–97,
  111–12
Monson, Thomas S., on
  friends, 110–11
Morality, 67–71, 111
Mormon, 11

Naaman, 62–63
Nelson, Russell M.,
  obedience of, 64–65

Nephi, 10, 17, 31–32, 35, 54–56

Oaks, Ann, 3
Oaks, Bart, 44–45
Oaks, Charles, 17–19
Oaks, Derek and Preot, 33–34
Oaks, Ethel, 87–88
Oaks, Gloria Unger, 3, 5, 32–33, 44, 108
Oaks, Kristie, 32–33, 95
Oaks, Perry and Marci, 42, 45–46
Oaks, Robert C.: fails to make BYU football team, 1–2; stung by wasp or hornet, 6; shot down in Vietnam, 24–27; refuses to drink vodka, 27–28; learns to trust in scriptures, 38–39; called to the Seventy, 46; trusts in F-111 fighter, 51–52; wrestles with origins of life, 59–60; blessed for paying tithing, 74–75; and story of grandfather, 78–79; and Word of Wisdom, 79–83; on blessings of service, 86–89; on blessings of missionary work, 95–97;

on marrying Gloria Unger, 108–9
Oaks, Wilbur, 87
Obedience: faith and, 49–56, 59–60; scriptures and, 60–64; Russell M. Nelson and, 64–65; Word of Wisdom and, 82–83; blessings and, 116–17
Ogilvie, James, 95

Peer pressure, 80–82
Perry, L. Tom, on education, 109
Plan of salvation, 13–14, 99–100
Pornography, Gordon B. Hinckley on, 111
Prayer, power of, 23–34
Prehistoric animals, 59–60
Priesthood, 11, 115
Prophet, the, 40–43

Repentance, 102
Revelation, continuing, 35–47
Romney, Marion G., on Atonement, 103–4
Rules, 13–14

Saul, 61–62
Scriptures: examples in, 21; trusting in, 36–39; faith

and, 54–56; obedience
and, 60–64

Seims, Richard, on
grandmother's conversion,
96–97

Service, 85–91, 117

Smith, Joseph, 11, 17, 31, 36,
38

Smith, Joseph Fielding, on
Atonement, 101–2

Strength, 24, 40, 110,
115–18

Temple, tithing and, 75–76

Thoughts, preceding action,
70–71

Thunderbirds, 4

Tithing, law of, 73–76

Trust: youth and, 11–15; in
arm of flesh, 17–21; in

prayer, 23–24; in prophets,
40–43; in the Spirit,
43–47; in arm of Lord,
115–19. *See also* Faith

Vietnam, author's prayer in,
24–27

Visiting teaching, 88–89

Vodka, story of, 27–28

Westenhaver, Joe, 25

Windshield wipers, story of,
33–34

Wine, 78

Wirthlin, Joseph B., on Word
of Wisdom, 110

Word of God, 35–47

Word of Wisdom, 27–28,
77–83, 110, 116

Youth, 9–15, 41, 67–68

About the Author

Elder Robert C. Oaks was called to the Second Quorum of the Seventy of The Church of Jesus Christ of Latter-day Saints in April 2000. As a general authority, he has served in the presidencies of the Africa Southeast Area and the Utah North Area.

Elder Oaks grew up in Provo, Utah, where he attended Brigham Young University before becoming a member of the first class of the United States Air Force Academy in 1955. Following his graduation, Elder Oaks completed U.S. Air Force pilot training and embarked on his military flying career as an F-100 Super Saber pilot, flying 188 combat missions in Vietnam. He was shot down over the Mekong Delta in 1966 but was rescued by U.S. Army helicopters. He was awarded the Distinguished Flying Cross and nine Air Medals for his service in Vietnam.

After receiving his master's degree in business administration from Ohio State University, Elder Oaks was assigned to the United States Air Force Academy, where he served as the Commandant's Executive for Honor and Ethics. He then returned to the cockpit, serving as a squadron commander in the swingwing F-111 Aardvark.

Elder Oaks was later assigned to the air staff in the Pentagon. Following his promotion to brigadier general, he commanded the 86th Tactical Fighter Wing at Ramstein, Germany, where he flew the F-4 Phantom fighter. Following his promotion to lieutenant general, he was assigned to Naples, Italy, where he commanded NATO Allied Air Forces in southern Europe. In this assignment, he flew the F-16 Falcon fighter.

Elder Oaks then commanded Air Training Command. In this assignment, he flew T-37 and T-38 jet trainers. In 1990, he was promoted to four-star rank and became commander of the United States Air Force in Europe and of NATO air forces in the central region of Europe.

For his service as a senior officer, Elder Oaks was awarded two Distinguished Service Medals. He is also the recipient of the U.S. Air Force Academy Association of Graduates Distinguished Graduate Award and the Brigham Young University Alumni Achievement Award. Following his retirement from the U.S. Air Force, he worked for US Airways as senior vice president over operations.

Before his call as a general authority, Elder Oaks served in a variety of callings, including stake president, Sunday School teacher, Young Men president, high councilor, and stake missionary.

Elder Oaks married Gloria Mae Unger in June 1959 in the Salt Lake Temple. They are the parents of six children.